They Chose Me

BY

DENISE LYNNETTE DEFOE

FOREWORD BY DR. EMORY J. TOLBERT

ISBN: 978-0-578-51336-2
Printed in the United States of America

Book design by Dalia I. Ibrahim
Cover design by Dalia I. Ibrahim

First Edition

DEDICATION

This book is dedicated to my sweet girl, Dayna Imara. You are the reason I chose to write this book. May my story convey to you the unwavering love I have for you. I find it an honor and a privilege to be your mother. You have shared my body and were lulled to sleep by my heartbeat. You are my flesh and blood and the only person I know that shares my DNA. I love you more than you will probably ever understand. I want so much for you but most of all I want you to be....unapologetically and authentically YOU.

To my remarkable husband David. You have poured more love into me than you know, and have given me a litany of reasons to be brave enough to do this. You are a prime example of persistence and commitment. Thank you for your unconditional love and ceaseless support of every single thing that I do. Thank you for accompanying me on this journey. I couldn't have done it without you. I love you so much.

TABLE OF CONTENTS

FOREWORD

As parents, nothing is more precious to us than our children. And some of us will get them in any and every way possible. This is a tradition among African Americans, who suffered for many years when our children could be sold away from us, or when we were sold away from them. During the horrible years of slavery, African Americans created make-shift families for children left behind at the slave market or sold to strangers apart from their parents. To this very day, virtually every Black family has extended child care and elder care to meet the needs of loved ones among us. As a result, foster care and adoption are familiar to us. The practice of extending our love beyond the traditional nuclear family is entirely normal and expected. Our beloved Denise entered our lives in 1981 when she was 15 months old. We were looking for a child to love in a special way. We expected our marriage to include children.When five years passed and none came, we looked within our family and then to various agencies for an opportunity to adopt. When the moment came, it was love at first sight. We had no particular image in mind, but we were sure that we would know when the opportunity came. Denise did not speak yet, but she reached for us during our first visit to the foster home where she lived. All of the paperwork and legal formalities took a while, but we were blessed to get her for keeps and to begin the long and happy journey of a lifetime. The fact that she was adopted was never kept from her. We preserved all of the photographs and documents of her life before and after she came to us in a scrapbook that she could see whenever she wished. We always emphasized the fact that she was entirely ours and we were entirely hers. To our delight, her development into an intelligent, thoughtful, friendly, balanced, self-directed and respectful daughter proceeded throughout her childhood and adolescence. She participated in church and community activities and did well in the private schools she attended from K through 12. She completed her Bachelors and Masters degrees and launched a successful career in social work. When she found an excellent husband we felt especially blessed. They gave us a precious granddaughter we are celebrating.

This book details some of the inner struggles that challenged Denise as an adopted child. Only she could share this story since we, as her parents, could not fully realize her perspective. She has taught us to be more sensitive to the emotional needs of our children, however they come to us and whatever the outward appearance might be. We are hoping that this book will be helpful to other adoptees, and that others looking to share the special blessing that comes with adopting a child will be encouraged. Denise is one of the joys of our life. We are so happy she is ours.

DR. EMORY TOLBERT, PH.D.

ACKNOWLEDGMENTS

I would first and foremost like to acknowledge my parents, Dr. Emory and Frances Tolbert. Your inimitable love for me cannot be put into words. You afforded me this amazing life and I am forever grateful that you chose me. Thank you to my sister Erin for being a sensational sister and a bold force to be reckoned with. I am extremely proud of all that you have accomplished. I love you all.

To the woman who gave me the courage to share my story with the world, Mrs. Beverly Robinson. You inspire me to stand within my purpose. Your own strength, resilience, and words of affirmation gave me exactly what I needed to put the pen to the paper. Thank you for your guidance and listening ear during this process. I cannot express how much I appreciate and love you.

To my sister friends. Thank you for pushing me beyond where I desire to go. You all were there when this book was birthed. Thank you for being my sounding board and reading and re-reading excerpts. Thank you for loving me, and for allowing me to be completely vulnerable and transparent with you. Amber, Carmen, Janelle, Porsche, Shalisha, and Tiffani.....I love you.

INTRODUCTION

This book has always been growing and radiating inside of me. It wasn't something that I tried to avoid, I just wasn't sure people would be interested in reading it. I allowed fear to convince me that the topic wasn't important. Over the years I wondered how I could in some way make an impact in this crazy world. I wondered what I had to contribute and how I could make a difference. Well, with the right people around me at the right time, this story came to life. Writing required me to dig deep within my own emotions to allow readers a glimpse into my experience as an adoptee. My hope is to give you an introspective look at my journey as I share the conflicting feelings that are so common among adoptees and the unique struggles that adoption presents them with. This book has changed me and I am thrilled to share this invaluable story with you. I am most grateful that *they chose me*...........

DENISE L. DEFOE
WASHINGTON, DC, 2019

One
JENISE

When a child is born, there is often a wave of excitement between the parents. Whether it was their first or their fourth, new parents can agree that the months leading up to the birth can be filled with nervousness, excitement, and joy. For typically forty weeks, mothers watch their bellies grow, expand, and create odd shapes as their fetus makes itself comfortable until just the right time. Family and friends join in the excitement with the new parents as they too prepare to meet the little person who has stolen their hearts. Baby registries, nursery preparation, name decisions, and baby showers are often the precursor to the moment when the child will arrive. Then delivery....watching the baby take its first breath, and hearing the first cry into a world that is so vast but full of love brings out a natural sense of elation that any new parent would feel. That was not the case for me.

On December 5, 1980 at 9:02 a.m. weighing in at 6lbs 2oz, Jenise Shacole Carter was born at University Hospital in San Diego, California. I'd like to believe that with Ilotycin coated eyes, whimpering newborn cries, and shivers from opioid withdrawal, she was able to see the face of her mother. Even if it was simply a glimpse. I always like to think that for just one passing moment, they locked eyes and the warmth of their bodies delicately touched as they embraced. I'd like to believe that gentle coos and cries would tug at the heart of her mother to reconsider the biggest decision of her entire life. I'd like to believe that whomever was at her bedside with her during her delivery was furiously coming up with ways to offer support and assistance to make motherhood work. But none of those things changed the course of that day. She left me there. Who would do that? The woman who carried me for nine months. The woman who felt me roll around in her stomach and kick her when I needed to stretch. The woman who laid down and made me. My own mother.

Brought into this world by no choice of my own...my own mother....left me. Let that sink in. I was abandoned at the time of my most vulnerable moments. When I needed her the most, suffering not only from withdrawal from the safety of her womb, but withdrawal from the choices she made with the substances she passed on to me. I was alone. They say that babies are very self-aware of their mothers immediately after birth. I wonder if I somehow knew I was by myself, with no one familiar to hug or nurse or hold me. While I may not have known what was actually going on, I wonder if I could sense the emptiness back then.

Stories suggest that she was incarcerated while pregnant with me, so I don't know if she returned to jail after she was discharged. I don't know if she found her way back to the streets. I don't know any of that. What I do know is that for 28 days I remained in University Hospital receiving treatment for opioid withdrawal. I wonder if I cried inconsolably, or was extremely fussy. Did I startle easily with stiff and rigid limbs whenever a loud noise erupted in the nursery? Was I experiencing difficulty with suckling to feed? Did I shake and twitch a lot as seen in many babies experiencing withdrawal? Was the staff finding it difficult to get me to go to sleep? I would like to believe that I was one of the babies that got held a little longer, and given a few more hugs since my biological tie was immediately severed. But who knows.

The story continues from there with many gaps that I am unable to fill. I was placed into foster care for two years until I was officially adopted. My adoptive parents thankfully kept most of my medical records, foster care case notes, adoption documents, and other important files. None of which had a name of anyone biologically connected to me, as they were not given that access. The papers were kept neatly and organized in albums around our house, and I had access to them whenever I wanted to peruse what little history of myself I could find and hang on to. It was all I had. My adoptive parents shared with me what little information they had and never kept any details from me when asked a question. Here are the things I was told:

My biological mother may have been 23 when she was pregnant with me.

My biological mother may have been a twin that I was named after.

I may have an older brother.

My biological mother may have been pregnant with me while incarcerated.

My biological mother had a history of substance abuse.

My biological mother's family may have attended the Baptist church up the street from the Seventh-Day Adventist church that I attended in San Diego.

That's all I knew for the majority of my life. I clung to these six small yet significant remnants of my life that connected me to something. Someone mysterious. I didn't know or care how accurate they were, I just kept them close in my heart as something that was all mine. Something that was about my lineage. That was all I had. Six probable facts and photos. Photos of me happily smiling around the age of 10 months old in the home of my foster mother, Mrs. Cobb. The photos show me with twin babies next to me playing on the floor, and other pictures of me randomly exploring the house that I currently have no recollection of.

Over the years, I made up narratives to go along with what was depicted in my photos. It was my way of filling the holes in my life I suppose. These fictitious tales brought me a sense of comfort to have some sort of story for my life. I fantasized that the twins shown in the pictures were my biological siblings, I mean hey, we KINDA looked alike...it could work. I imagined that we were somehow separated from our biological mother and that my foster mother Mrs. Cobb was my biological grandmother. I'm more than sure that is not how the story went, but that is what I chose to create in my mind. I don't know if the twins were foster kids, or if they were relatives of Mrs. Cobb and it doesn't even matter. They were my sisters in my head. It allowed me to create my own little family. My own little story.

Mrs. Cobb was the only foster mother I was placed with. I don't know how she was chosen, or how I got to her. I have no memories of being in foster care at all. I guess I'm thankful for that. So many foster children have quite colorful experiences being bounced from foster home to foster home, never having a sense of stability. Others are exposed to traumatic experiences from the living conditions of the foster home, to treatment from other foster kids and parents, and overall care. I'd like to believe that my foster home experience was wonderful and that I was treated with love and care until my adoption was made official in 1983.

As far back as I can remember, I've known I was adopted. It was never a secret or a shocking revelatory story that my adoptive parents sat me down for, followed by anger and resentment like you would see on television. It was always something that was a part of me. I'm glad it happened that way. I don't remember how the conversation went, or what age I was actually told. I don't know how it even came up. I do remember asking them how they chose me. As a child I always envisioned a "child pound" filled with sad faced, unkempt orphans in the window looking pitiful and longing for homes. I envisioned myself sitting in the corner, with my head down patiently waiting to be picked. I remember humming to myself on several occasions the tune of

"How Much is that Doggie in The Window".....replacing the word "doggie" with "child". When I shared this with my adoptive parents, I was told that my depiction was pretty inaccurate.

My adoptive parents explained to me that a few years after they married, they decided that they were ready to have children. After having a devastating ectopic pregnancy, they decided to explore the route of adoption. They enrolled in the foster to adopt program through the Teyari Adoption Agency. This agency was created for foster parents who were solely interested in adopting African American children. Workshops, home studies, and pre and post adoptive literature were given to these individuals who desired to adopt the child and not remain the foster parent. My adoptive parents initially started out fostering a little boy around the age of 5 named, well let's just call him "Q". He was quite mischievous and had a quirky spirit I'm told. My adoptive parents initially really wanted a boy, but I believe "Q" was a bit more than they were ready for. After an attempt to set the house on fire, they decided that it was no longer a safe fit for them.

They returned to Teyari and met with their caseworker. She stated to them that she knew they were interested in adopting a boy but they had the perfect little girl for them. She exited the room and re-entered with me dressed in a yellow dress, bobby socks, and white bows in my hair. My adoptive parents immediately fell in love. They gushed over me and knew they had to have me. Paperwork started, and they began to foster me on the weekends in their home. During the week, I remained with Mrs. Cobb.

When I was around the age of 1, I began staying with my adoptive parents from Friday evening to Sunday to begin integrating me into their schedule and routine. It was an opportunity to see if everything was a good fit. I can only liken this experience to purchasing a new car and test driving it. I was like their new car and they were going to decide if they were going to take me off the lot for good. I'm sure that going from a pyromaniac to an infant was quite a change of pace for them, but they were up for the challenge. Every Friday my adoptive parents would pick me up from Mrs. Cobb's house for our weekend visits. My adoptive mother told me she always looked forward to Fridays. She loved coming to get me and take me to their home. She said she really enjoyed dressing me up and showering me with toys and love.

My adoptive parents said that over time, they would come to pick me up from Mrs. Cobb's house and I began reaching for them as if I was ready to "go home". They believed I knew my foster home wasn't permanent and that I was demonstrating that I really truly liked being with them. I wonder if it made Mrs. Cobb feel some kind of way. As an adult I learned that she tried to stop my adoption. She wanted to keep me as her foster child. Maybe she really loved me and couldn't bear to see me go.....or maybe I was simply a paycheck. Who knows. She is deceased now, and I will never have that answer. Thankfully her attempts did not work.

Many weekly check-ins and home visits were conducted by Teyari and Social Services to ensure that the home of the people who wanted to be my parents, the people who wanted to call me daughter, the people who wanted to give me a permanent home, the people who wanted ME...was safe, stable, nurturing, and full of love. Everything checked out and the adoption process ensued. The woman that birthed me, then left me shivering and alone in a sterile hospital room, had most likely moved on with her life. For me, my new life had just begun.

Two

DENISE

It was a sunny afternoon, a day that would change my life forever. Friday July 8, 1983 was the date. It was the day that my adoption was made official. I finally had parents of my own. It was so much more than that. It was also the day that I transitioned from being all alone in a world where I did not belong, to having an instant family. Parents of my own, grandparents, cousins, aunts, relatives. All of my own. I was no longer required to be a nomad, meandering back and forth to Mrs. Cobb's house. No more weekend suitcases and no more wondering if the lovely couple who treated me so well were going to come back and get me, and carry me off again to a place that I knew was so full of fun and love. I had a home that would soon be my permanent place of living. As an energetic two year old, I did not truly understand the significance and magnitude of what this day meant. If I could put my present self in my past shoes, I imagine I felt liberating, warm, and intimate.

I often wondered as a teen what that day looked like as I left Mrs. Cobb for good. Was she upset that she wasn't able to stop my adoption? Was she genuinely sad to see me go? How did the other children respond to me leaving? I will never have these answers, but they have crossed my mind. I'm sure there were other kids in the foster home that I came from that had not been adopted yet, and they may or may not have had prospects. Did I display emotion about leaving them? I'm sure I didn't fully grasp that I was not coming back to them. I do know one thing, I now had a family. Two people who committed to shift their entire world to fit me in it. Dr. Emory and Frances Tolbert chose me. I was now their daughter.

We went to the San Diego Courthouse and stood before Judge Joseph. My Godparents Calvin and Paradine Ruff were in attendance to support my parents in this joyous occasion. I love looking at the pictures from this day. The smiles are so bright and you can literally see the love jump from the page. We were all dressed to perfection. I believe my mom wanted me to look extra special on "adoption day" as I had on a pink satin dress with white ruffle trim. In one picture, I appear to be scratching my neck; that lace was likely itchy. I looked pretty nonetheless in my lace church socks, white patent leather shoes, and two white bows in my neatly brushed hair. The picture quality of the 80s is less than stellar. No filters or brightening. No digital clarity or high definition quality. It's ok, though because what we have is perfect. Everyone signed on the dotted line, and immediately I had a family.

My name was officially changed from Jenise Shacole Carter to Denise Lynnette Tolbert soon after I was adopted. My mom didn't care for the "J" so she switched it to "D" and gave me her middle name. As a child I loved having the same middle name as my mom. It gave me a sense that I belonged. I mean how special is it that my mom would give me her name. For a while I loved it, but as time wore on I began to question why it was necessary to change my name at all. Was there something wrong with the one I was given? Was it not good enough? Was someone trying to rob me of my biological identity? It made me upset that this piece of my history was erased. Were they trying to erase my past? I remember as a child, doodling my birth name on sheets of paper in my Trapper Keeper notebooks that I used for school. It was my way of relishing the memory of the name given to me at birth. It was the only original piece of me that I had. I knew no one else's name in my biological family, but I knew mine. I knew I was a Carter. I had no idea what that meant, what stigma was attached to it, or familial history connected to the name, but it was mine. It was speculated that I was named after my biological mother's twin sister. So was my biological mother's name Denise? I often wondered if they had common twin rhyming names. If so, then it's pretty cool that I have her name now if that's even true. It could just be another memory I created since there is no proof of either of their names. Where on earth did Shacole come from? What was the origin of that name? Did my father have any say in naming me? Why did my biological mom even waste the time naming me if she wasn't going to keep me anyway? I'll never understand that. Did she hope they would keep the name she gave me? Was she hopeful it was a way she could find me in the future? Whatever her reason, my name was taken away. It was another piece of my life that was replaced. The grief from "losing" my name was unexplainable. I felt almost ashamed that my biological name wasn't considered or acknowledged as a significant piece of who I was.

Who IS Denise? Is she truly this person who is an outgoing extrovert who really loves crowds and being the center of attention? Are her insecurities the same that Jenise would have dealt with or are they a RESULT of being adopted? Are my natural responses to anger, confrontation, embarrassment, or guilt...responses that are biologically within me or are they conditioned responses due to my upbringing? Did my true identity mold and conform to what was shown to me in my environment? What biological character traits do I still possess? Am I stubborn like my biological father? Am I passive like my maternal grandmother? Am I bold like my brother? Am I afraid to fail like my biological mother? These questions consumed my thoughts more than anything else. Who on earth did I identify with? I'll never know.

Perhaps I am grateful for the person I became following my name change. It took many years of hard work, personal reflection, and professional help for me to begin to feel like my true authentic self. Identity formation for me was a long process because of all of the questions about my family of origin. It took quite some time for me to realize that I did not have to change who I was to accommodate people in order for them to like me enough not to leave me. It was difficult to arrive at the place where I began to see my adoption for the blessing that it was, and even the role my new name played in the person I became. I began to realize that even though my name was changed without my permission, it was the catalyst to reshaping my entire purpose and future on this earth. It created an environment of permanency, safety, unconditional love, and acceptance. This allowed me to explore my feelings, build character, and gain an inner strength to form a new identity.

Jenise Shacole Carter may have had a destiny much differently designed than Denise Lynnette Tolbert, and I am glad that I was given a chance to figure out what that destiny is. I am glad for the second chance at life. I am grateful for the opportunity to have been raised in a home full of love, with parents willing to do whatever it took to give their little girl all the love they could give. Jenise Shacole Carter may have been my name given to me at birth, but Denise Lynnette Tolbert had become the name I needed to let me know that I would not be abandoned. It confirmed that I belonged and was valued. It solidified that I was accepted and not rejected. I am so thankful that I was able to say goodbye to Jenise Shacole Carter, and embrace the new name that my parents chose for me, the name they chose to make me their own.

Three
WE ARE A FAMILY

I am very proud to be the daughter of two simply remarkable people. I was never made to feel as if I didn't belong. They were the only parents I knew, and I was their daughter. *They chose me.* I used to wonder how my parents told their family and friends about their decision to adopt and how people reacted when I just appeared. It must have been pretty exciting for them. I remember flipping through the old photo albums and seeing several "Congratulations on your adoption" greeting cards in them. That was thoughtful of people. My mom told me that there were quite a few families in our church in San Diego who had adopted children from the same agency they used to adopt me. So for my parents and their friends, I was just another kid to love. My cousins recently told me that I was just another cousin to love. None of them ever cared that I was adopted. There were so many grandkids, I just fell right into the mix.

My parents were childhood sweethearts, literally, they grew up together. Their families were very close. Both of them were born in Sanford, Florida and lived in the same neighborhood. My mom always says that my dad was truly "the boy next door". My mom the oldest of eight children, and my dad the youngest of three, have extensive stories about their childhoods and what shaped them into who they are today. My father's parents fostered many children when he was a child. Many were adopted by other families, but two were officially adopted by his parents. The empathy that my grandparents had by creating a home for children that did not have one, I believe was instilled in dad at a very young age. This compassion continued inside of him.

Both of my parents grew up in the Seventh-Day Adventist church and remained very active in various committees and departments within their local church. My parents are both educators, so the importance of education and developing a solid career were values instilled in me at a very early age. My mom worked in the school system for over forty years, several years in the classroom, and finally retiring as a highly respected school administrator in the role of a Principal. It wasn't until her retirement party that I was able to fully understand how revered she was by former students, staff members, and colleagues. She was simply "Mommy" to me. To see such admiration for her made me extremely proud.

My father pursued a career on the collegiate and graduate levels. He taught several undergraduate courses and served as the Chairman of the History Department at Howard University for ten years. His love for history began his collection of historical books, magazines, manuscripts, and music which now spans to an impressively unmatched home library of over 20,000 books and relics bragging of African American history. Growing up, his library was always just another part of the house. I don't believe I truly understood or appreciate the black excellence that surrounded me. It was a space that I always enjoyed sitting in, and joining in on tours of it when people came over. My dad has always been so humble about the contents of his library, and it wasn't until I was an adult that I recognized what I was in the midst of. He is a living legend who makes it his mission to educate others about a history that has often been muddled with lies and inaccuracies....and he is my dad. I am such a lucky girl.

With both of my parents being educators, they were pretty busy during the summers while I was on break from school, so they kept me busy. I vividly remember being toted around to my dad's summer school Undergraduate classes at Cal State Fullerton and UCLA. I sat through many classes and lectures on the African Diaspora and Chicano Studies. When my attention in his classes wandered, he would simply take me to his office where I could watch VHS tapes of old episodes of Amos N' Andy, Beulah, and Eyes on the Prize. I'm sure I'm the only 8 year old in the 1980's who loved those shows. After his classes, my dad would sometimes treat me to a trip to Knotts Berry Farm or Disneyland. I enjoyed going with him to work.

My mom made sure I remained involved in a host of activities during the summers filled with educational enrichment with focus on drama, calligraphy, creative writing, and foreign language. I remember her wanting to expose me to the arts and music to keep my mind stimulated and engaged in learning. I recall enjoying weeks of camps for kids interested in Marine Biology at SeaWorld in San Diego which fueled my love for marine life, primarily dolphins. I was pretty active in church as a choir member, Pathfinder, and Usher. I attended wonderful private schools and obtained a wonderful education. I made exceptional friends and made strong connections with indescribable mentors. I lived in beautiful homes and I truly lacked for nothing. I had a wonderful childhood in San Diego. I was given more than I could have ever imagined or asked for. I was pretty spoiled; not rotten, just spoiled. My parents did everything that they could to ensure that I knew I was a member of their family. I was never treated any differently by them or made to feel that I was somehow an external member brought in. Feeling included and a part of their unit was something they did well, I never knew anything else.

I would not say I grew up in a very strict household. There were rules, and consequences for not following those rules, but everything was given within reason. I was grounded quite a bit in high school because I didn't complete a homework assignment, or because I didn't follow through with doing my chores. I was always punished for something valid. However, at the time, it sucked. I received minimal spankings. I was grounded more times than I choose to remember but I digress. I am thankful for the discipline that I received (now). Rules are necessary. Boundaries are necessary. I often wondered what my life would have been like had I remained with my biological mother. Did I have an attitude like her? Would she abuse drugs and alcohol around me? Would I be punished for things that she herself did? Would I be punished for the decisions she made? These are just a few of the questions that invaded my mind as a teen. I was a typical teenager. I had typical mood swings, typical talking back, and typical rebellion. I'm sure that ages 13-17 were probably not the most favorite years for my parents, but we endured and made it through. Now that I'm a mother, I am curious to see what my daughter's teenage years will be like. I am eager to see which characteristics of me and her father will come out through her. Who am I kidding.....I am scared.

In talking with other adoptees, some revealed how they always had an internal struggle with feeling like they had to do and be their best to ensure they wouldn't be taken back to wherever they came from. They knew that would never happen, but they always felt like they had to be their "best" to prove to their adoptive parents they made a good decision with getting them in the first place. I never felt that way, and I find it interesting that they did. It just goes to show that everyone internalizes their adoption very differently.

Although my family did everything possible to ensure that I knew I was loved and a part of their family, I still longed for a biological connection. I didn't even really recognize it at the young age of eleven. I remember on occasion while we lived in San Diego, walking around the grocery store, the mall, the roller skating rink, pretty much anywhere we went, looking for someone that I thought looked like me; anyone. I remember staring in people's faces to see if they had the same features as me, looking at people's posture to see if they had the same mannerisms as me, listening out for voices to see if they sounded like me. I needed to find someone that was out there that I could link to my biological family. Again, I was eleven, so I didn't quite understand what I was doing, or where this longing was coming from. I wasn't even able to encapsulate and express how I was feeling. But I imagined that I would just stumble upon a family member while being out and about and we both would just KNOW who we each were, and that we were family. I imagined that we would hug and cry and they would immediately want to get to know me and be a part of my life. It sounded foolproof in my head, but it never happened.

I loved living in San Diego. I knew two seasons: Spring and Summer. The weather was always perfect and the beach was a drive away. I have awesome memories of eating exquisite, barbeque food at Love's BBQ Pit with my mom after a long day at work. We ordered the same thing every time we went. The waitresses would roll a glass cart filled with desserts for us to choose from after dinner. I wanted to work there so badly. I loved the hustle and bustle of the restaurant which was always full. I also enjoyed going to the Del Mar Fair with my family and riding on the rides and winning oversized stuffed animals as prizes to ring toss and skee-ball. My mom used to go to a hair salon called Beau Monde and would tote me around with her per usual. Going to the salon was always a fun experience. Her stylist was Miss M. She was a short black woman with a mole over the top of her lip on the right hand side. I would sit in the back room of the salon where the towels and hair dye were stored. While there, I would sometimes do homework, help fold freshly dried towels, or listen to rap on my Walkman....unbeknownst to my mom. There is where my love for Ice Cube began. Miss M. would occasionally come back to the back room to grab a towel and sneak a drag from her cigarette. Leaving bright pink lipstick around the rim of cigarette, she would put it down in the ashtray and place a finger to her lips as to shush me since she knew she was supposed to smoke outdoors. She was always very intriguing and could DO hair! I loved being her helper by sweeping up hair around the shampoo bowl. That was a big job for a ten year old. San Diego was filled with so many memories that I will forever cherish. A phone call that my dad received one day changed everything.

In 1991 my father was appointed the Chairman of the History Department at Howard University which required us to move from San Diego, California to the Maryland area. He ended up moving first while my mom and I stayed behind until the house sold and our school years were over. We joined him in the summer of 1992. Moving from California was quite traumatic for me. I was leaving all that I ever knew;

friends, church, school, and extracurricular activities. My entire foundation was there. I was terrified to leave it all. What if I couldn't rebuild that network in Maryland? What if people rejected me because I was the new girl from the West Coast? What if my biological family wanted to look for me? They wouldn't know where I was. How would they find me if I left? What if my biological family had someone secretly keeping tabs on me? I couldn't tell them where I was going. Imagine that, I was afraid to leave people behind that I didn't even know. How on earth would this work? All of these questions exhausted me for months. After things got settled and we established a routine, I realized things weren't as bad as I thought they would be. I ended up beginning middle school at an awesome school. I began making new school and church friends, and getting pretty involved in extracurricular activities. The fantasy continued that I would randomly run into a family member in Maryland although deep down I knew it was impossible. I knew that the biological family that I longed for and hoped I would stumble across in the streets of San Diego couldn't possibly just randomly be in the same state, city, and town that I lived in in Maryland. It didn't even make sense, but at the time it was very real to me.

I was an only child for 12 years of my life. In May of 1992 my sister Erin was born to my mother's sister Barbara. Unfortunately, two weeks after Erin's birth, Aunt Barbara passed away. My aunts rallied together to care for Erin and my mom ultimately made the decision to officially adopt her. I had a little sister! It was exciting and scary at the same time. Up until this time, it had just been me, my mom, and dad. All of the attention had been focused on me and what I wanted and needed. But now with a new baby entering the mix I wondered what it would mean for our family. How were things going to change? During this time, we had just relocated from San Diego, CA to Silver Spring, MD. There was so much transition happening and now we were adding an infant to the mix?

Growing up with a little sister was fun. When she was a baby, she was MY baby. I enjoyed preparing bottles for her and helping change her and get her ready for bed. I toted her around when she was a toddler and I loved playing with her. Having a 12-year age difference was challenging at times because by the time she was entering elementary school I was already in high school and soon off to college. So our relationship really blossomed after she went to high school. I never really talked to her about being adopted. For years I didn't have a true handle on how I felt about my own adoption, let alone finding out how she felt about hers.

I often envied Erin. I envied the fact that even after being adopted she still knew her biological family. She has an older biological sister, and a host of nieces and nephews that are all accessible to her. She had people that she could identify with. People who resembled her. She had a biological connection to who she is. At any time she could sit at the feet of family members and hear stories about who her mother was and what kind of person she was. She could hear about the ways she was like her mother. I longed for that connection. That kind of access. I was always so proud that our family stepped up to ensure that she remained within the family and didn't get bounced around in the foster care system.

I remember feeling alone and disassociated when my friends and family would share stories about their own conception, mother's pregnancy, and their own births. I had no one to laugh with about what I was like as a newborn. Who I spit up on, what soothed me, how I fell asleep to certain songs. It felt like I was looking in a glass house from the outside. I never, ever felt included in those conversations. No one knew that though. My personality allowed those painful feelings to be covered up and never acknowledged. I remember one Thanksgiving in Rochester, NY where my parents grew up, and most of my family still resides. We were having dinner at an aunt's house and my cousins were engaged in a stirring conversation about being babies and newborn pics scattered around the house we were in. I remember secretly removing myself cerebrally from the conversation. I kind of just tuned everyone out as jabs went back and forth about who was a "bad" baby and who was a "creepy looking" baby. I remember us all looking at a group picture of our entire family at the very first family reunion that was hosted by my mom's family. I was around 2 or 3. That was my earliest picture with all of my cousins who were all around the same age. I don't even remember how me being adopted came into the conversation on that particular day. All of my cousins knew I was adopted since day one, but I remember my cousin Dawan declaring after dinner, "Yo, that doesn't even matter. We FAMILY. We all family. It ain't about how you get here. We just family. That's it." It startled me for a minute as I tuned back into the conversation, and we all just kinda sat there. Some cousins nodded in agreement murmuring, "Mmm-hmm" or "That's right".

From that point on I never seemed to feel weird during those conversations anymore. I just felt loved. Don't get me wrong, nothing prior to that day made me feel any less loved, but his declaration kinda sealed their love for me even more. I no longer felt like a puzzle piece that didn't fit.

Four

HAPPY BIRTHDAY

Pinatas, clowns, sleepovers, skating parties, Chuck E. Cheese, costume parties, I had it all. I LOVED MY BIRTHDAY! All my life my parents saw to it that I had great parties and received lots of gifts. There was never a year that I did not celebrate with friends and family, minus the year that I caught the chicken pox from my sister Erin. I loved being the center of attention and partying hard for my birthday. I loved celebrating another year and having people sing to me and shower me with love just for being born. However, they were and are still very difficult. It is like there was some sort of distant traumatic memory built into my psyche that sends me into a state of reflection and introspection. It's a trigger of sorts. Remembering that this was the day I possibly said goodbye to my biological mother forever.

It wasn't until I was a teenager that birthdays became really hard for me. I remember vividly on my 14th birthday sitting on my bed, wrapped in my robe looking out of my bedroom window. It was a full moon and I just sat there staring into space. Tears welled up into the brim of my eyelids and I began to silently weep. I believe listening to Mariah Carey's song "Miss You Most (At Christmas Time)" didn't help. I remember the feeling that consumed me while sitting against the backboard of my bed. Sadness and loneliness enveloped me. What came next was something I didn't know was inside of me. I began speaking out loud. I asked the sky which served as a proxy for the biological mother that I did not know,

"I wonder if you're thinking about me."

"I'm turning 14 today, do you even care?"

"Do you think about me on my birthday, the day you chose to get rid of me?"

"Is this day hard for you?"

"Do you regret not being here celebrating with me?"

"Do you even remember me?"

Question after question left my mouth. As I spoke, more tears flooded my face. I needed to ask the space these questions. I had to. They were questions that no one had the answers to anyway. So why not ask invisible mommy in the sky like a weirdo. Every year from that day forward I did this. It sure made me feel better. It was my own annual emotional outburst. The tears and vocalization of my feelings allowed me to free myself of emotions and questions that I had no idea what to do with. For a short moment, and only in these moments, anger and resentment left my body. I only wished that she missed me and was thinking about me as much as I thought about and missed her on that specific date. It was a date that we shared. Surely she didn't forget me. Certainly she remembers giving birth to me. Maybe she acts like the day never existed. She can't....that's impossible! Do other people around her remember it? Do they remind her of the child she left in the hospital? She was my human incubator. December 5 had to affect her as much as it affected me. But maybe it never did. It hurt to imagine that. It stung, and it literally made my heart hurt.

Although most of my birthdays were spent celebrating in some fashion surrounded by so many friends and family members....I remember often feeling very alone at times. The parties were just a way of distracting myself with a temporary means of keeping the day upbeat and not filled with tears. No one could understand what I was feeling on my birthdays, and nothing could be done to change my feelings despite what I did to manage them.

I've spoken to other adoptees who have shared with me that outside of their birthdays, other holidays were pretty somber for them. For some, Mother's Day and Father's day were extremely painful because it reminded them of a person who abandoned them. For others, celebrating Thanksgiving and Christmas, the holidays where family comes together the most, was particularly difficult. Some have said being around the family they were given and not the family they were born into on specific holidays made them feel exactly how I feel on my birthday. It never crossed my mind on any of those days. However, I can understand why and how the adoptee may feel on what is normally a joyous and celebratory event.

As I have gotten older and through my healing journey, my birthday has become less "somber". I still have a weight of self- reflection and introspection that lays heavily on my spirit at some point throughout the day. The day triggers something within me. Maybe somewhere deep inside my mind and body elicits this response and reaction because of the traumatic experience of being relinquished. I don't really know. My husband and close friends know I need "my time" to still emote. I still to this day I speak to my sky proxy of a biological mother. I still speak to an unresponsive sky to remind myself how this day changed my entire life. It changed my entire destiny. My purpose. The day is much less tear filled for me as

I have been able to fully understand my feelings about being adopted and how it has shaped me as a person.

I have always been able to repress certain feelings and memories that I choose not to remember whether they were related to trauma or because I didn't like how they made me feel. I never recognized it until I was older, but certain things that I watched on television would stir up feelings within me that I was sure was discarded in my "Let's not think about this" bank. Even certain music that I listened to would evoke emotions that I had hoped to forget and surely didn't want to uncover again as it related to being adopted.

One of my girlfriends and I had a weekly date to watch the Hulu television series "The Handmaid's Tale". Every Wednesday we endured this captivatingly torturous show with sheer fear with each episode. By phone we would text screams of horror or send real time pictures of our faces in disbelief of what we had just witnessed on the show or what was to come on the upcoming episode.

One episode in particular aired during Season 2. It was episode 10: The Last Ceremony. As usual our hearts were being dragged across the ground and our mouths dropped at the horrendous rituals executed within the episode. But one particular scene literally brought me to my knees; tears, snot, and audible weeping crippled me. I watched the main character "Offred" played by Elisabeth Moss go on a secret trip to see her daughter who had been forcibly taken from her due to barbaric rules in the town of Gilead that the show portrays. In the scene, "Offred's" daughter Hannah wasn't terribly happy to see her mother. Being separated now for what the show depicted as several months, Hannah had been given a new name and entered into a new family as was the custom in the setting of the dystopian and dark show. Hannah who now goes by the name Agnes asked her mother, "Did you look for me?" "Offred" replies, "Every day." The child then proceeds to explain that she had been given new parents. Offred wept trying to make sense of it all while relishing the few minutes that were granted to her to spend with her daughter. As the time of this secret encounter was ending, "Offred's" last words to her daughter were, "enjoy your life. Love your parents."

This scene pierced me as I wept and thought to myself, "I wonder what kind of conversation my biological mother had with me before she turned me over to the hospital staff. Were her eyes filled with tears? Did she speak words of encouragement over me? What were her last words to me? Were they similar to what Offred said to her daughter?" God, I wish I could remember. Maybe she just handed me to a nurse and rolled over. I don't like to envision that as a possibility, but it could be.

I remembered a dream I had many years ago about my biological mother. I remember being in a room and she walked in. I didn't realize it was her, but she knew it was me. I may have been about 16 at the time I dreamt it, but I seemed younger in my actual dream. The woman didn't say a word to me. She simply walked up to me and hugged me. I immediately knew who she was. As we embraced with tear stained cheeks I whispered in her ear, "Why did you leave me? Why did you give me away? Have you been looking for me?" She told me that she never stopped looking for me and that she was so sorry that she couldn't take care of me. She apologized profusely over and over. It made me feel good to have those answers. To hear her acknowledge that she couldn't take care of me gave me understanding. Well it did while I was still sleeping. I knew once I woke up none of it would be real. I wanted to stay asleep because this was all a dream. But alas, morning came. I remember that dream so vividly, although I tried to forget it.

In recent years, I dreamed that I went to San Diego. I had gotten in contact with someone who knew my biological family. This person got in contact with them and informed them that I would be flying into town. I remember deplaning and going up an escalator to baggage claim. There was a small group of about 5 or 6 people waiting at the top. As soon as I saw them I fell to my knees and sobbed. I saw a woman who looked just like me. I was hysterically crying as she walked towards me hand in hand with an elderly woman who happened to be my grandmother. The woman who looked just like me approached me and said, "I am not your mother, but I am her twin. Your mother passed several years ago." It didn't even matter to me in the dream. I was just so happy to meet them. I remember waking up from that dream sweating and crying. It was such a heartfelt moment. I cherished every minute of that dream. Maybe that dream will one day come true.

Five
THE SEARCH

I remember it like it was yesterday. I was sitting in after school care waiting for my mom to pick me up from San Diego Academy in San Diego, California where I attended elementary school. I had to be about eight or nine years old at the time. There were kids outside playing tetherball and handball on the black top. Some ran around the playground, and the rest of us sat crowded around a huge SHARP TV/VCR combination unit. The movie we watched was the 1982 version of "Annie". I remember gazing at the screen as the red headed orphan sang out of her window at the Hudson Street Home For Girls. The song "Maybe" blasted from the screen and my eyes filled with tears as the lyrics written by Martin Charnin went like this:

THEY CHOSE ME

Maybe far away
Or maybe real nearby
He may be pouring her coffee
She may be straightening his tie!
Maybe in a house
All hidden by a hill
She's sitting playing piano,
He's sitting paying a bill!
Betcha they're young
Betcha they're smart
Bet they collect things
Like ashtrays, and art!
Betcha they're good
(Why shouldn't they be?)
Their one mistake
Was giving up me!
So maybe now it's time,
And maybe when I wake
They'll be there calling me "Baby"
Maybe.
Betcha he reads
Betcha she sews
Maybe she's made me
A closet of clothes!
Maybe they're strict
As straight as a line
Don't really care
As long as they're mine!
So maybe now this prayer's
The last one of its kind...

Won't you please come get your "Baby"
Maybe

A mix of feelings welled up within me. Feelings that I had no idea what to do with. Feelings that I had never experienced before. I was that orphan in the window asking those questions. I shared the same questions and sentiments as Annie. Those lyrics resonated with me and left me speechless. Questions began to swirl in my head. I decided not to do anything with them out of fear of the unknown. For years I tucked them deep down and chose to forget them. I allowed them to stack and stack without any place to go. I didn't know who to talk to about them and I didn't know if what I was feeling was normal. I mean why would anyone want to hear my questions about people who chose to give me away? Who cares what they're doing? They don't care what I am doing. Or do they? To this day the song "Maybe" fills the brim of my eyes with tears. Occasionally some still fall. It's a powerful song.

I never wanted my biological parents to come get me. I never wanted to leave my home and the only family that I've ever known. However, the questions and desire to know who I was and understand where I came from only began to stir deeper within me as I became a teenager. As I got more "smart-mouthed" and rebellious, I was rightfully grounded and reprimanded. I would often inaudibly mutter, "I wonder what my REAL mother would have done in this situation." I always imagined that her response to my deviance would be much less strict and less consequential. I sometimes hoped she wouldn't care and I could do as I pleased. I would have NEVER asked that inaudible question out loud, but it crossed my mind. I'm glad it stayed in my head.

During the summers as a teen while school was out of session I found myself noticing a new trend on many of my favorite talk shows. Reuniting long lost family members was a topic I couldn't seem to escape when flipping through the channels. Whether it was an adoptee looking for their biological parents, or an estranged family reconnecting after many years, it didn't matter. Every show of this kind had me crying buckets before the credits rolled. Buckets. I don't know why I continued to torture myself by watching them, but I did. It gave me some sort of hope. Maybe my biological family was tuned in at that same moment and wanted to reunite! Maybe they had been looking for me this entire time! Maybe not. The people on these shows found their family members from everywhere! Contracted professionals gathered as much data as possible to reunite these families and bring healing and closure. It sounded perfect! I remember taking down phone numbers to these talk shows so that I could call in and be a guest. I recall a few episodes where the family members didn't want to be found or couldn't be found for one reason or another. Those episodes were extremely devastating to me. I remember wondering, "What if I actually call in to the talk show and they find my family? What if they are ones that don't want to be found? What if they don't want to explain their decision for giving me up? I just went on NATIONAL TELEVISION only to be rejected AGAIN. This time in front of millions of people." I always wondered how these reunions really affected the guests coming on. For close to 50 minutes, viewers got to see several prettily packaged reunion experiences. But what happens next? Did the families stay in contact? Were they just one big happy family now? Were there other family members from the reunion that didn't want to be contacted or bothered? What about the individuals that went on and didn't have a successful outcome from the show? How did they go on? I can't even imagine. What an emotional toll all of this must have played on both sides of the reunion. I remember one particular reunion show that flashed a huge phone number at the bottom of the screen: 1-800-BIG-HUGS. I wrote it down and tucked it in my diary just in case I decided to call. Everyone who called them seemed to have so much success in finding their estranged loved ones.

In 1997, I wrote Oprah a fourteen-page letter front and back pleading with her to find my biological family. I just knew that if anyone could find my family, it would be Oprah. The idea of going on her show outshined the actual idea of meeting my long-lost family. Getting a chance to meet OPRAH?!? I would be the talk of the town. I imagined her becoming so enamoured with my story that we stayed in contact for years to come. Just me, her, and Gayle King. I shared this with a few friends of mine who begged to go with me if I ever got on. I remember trying to decide which ones I would bring with me on the show for "moral support" or "20 seconds of fame". Over time, I revised my letter adding more details and taking out irrelevant pieces. The longer I held onto it, the more nervous I became. I couldn't bear the idea of sending my heartfelt letter and never hearing from Oprah. What if she never gets the letter? What if it's one that she isn't terribly impressed with? But what if she DOES get the letter and she ends up telling me that she couldn't find my family. What if I get chosen to be on the show and I end up being denied by my family on national television like some previous guests of other shows in the past. I couldn't let that happen. I would be humiliated. Nerves got the best of me and 2 years later I tore the letter up. I never uttered a word about it to my parents, and my friends never brought it up again.

I was always curious about the woman who gave birth to me. I was worried at times that my parents may feel as though I didn't feel loved enough by them. I was afraid they would question why I felt the need to search. I remember going back and forth about talking with my parents about my desire to find my biological mother. Would they be mad? Would this hurt them? Would they feel betrayed? Would they treat me differently? Would they even help? The guilt consumed me for years. I told myself to just chill. I reminded myself that I was "chosen and special". How selfish of me to want to find people who didn't even want me. "Just shut up and be grateful, Denise". This was the narrative that played in my head. But the feeling wouldn't go away. No matter how hard I tried to repress them, the desire grew. I grieved a family I did not know. The sadness would come in waves, and I had no clue how to deal with it. It was a loss of identity, a loss of culture, a loss of a familial tie. The bond severed for me at childbirth needed to be explained. I needed, no I deserved to know WHY. I talked with them about it and they were completely open with whatever questions I had. I wanted to do the search alone and at my own pace. They willingly gave me the freedom to do just that.

When I was about 17 years old I took a deep breath, walked down to the basement, sat on the couch with my dad and just asked. "Do you know anything about my biological family?" He proceeded to tell me as many details as he had. I was filled. Each detail put me a bit closer to my mysterious identity. What he had wasn't much but it was enough for me at that time. He directed me to my adoption paperwork and photo albums and encouraged me to search. He made himself available for any further questions I had. I took the albums and I studied them. I read and re-read case notes from my foster home. I took everything I could find and laid it on the basement floor absorbing it all; trying to piece everything together, attempting to make sense of it all. I felt like a private investigator. Every day my interest peaked more and more as well as my anxiety. I thought, "OMG!!! WHAT IF I ACTUALLY FIND THESE PEOPLE!!!" Fear gushed my mind. "What if they are mad that I found them? What if they want me back?" ALL of these negative thoughts overpowered my decision to search. The fear of rejection was too great. I couldn't handle it. What if it destroyed me? How would I go on? It was all too much for this 17 year old so I put the search on hold for a couple of months.

It was July of 1998, and I decided to whip out my baby albums and adoption papers again. I sat on the floor of the basement, this time with the phone number to University Hospital in my hands. I trembled as I dialed the number. A kind woman answered the phone and said, "Good Afternoon, University Hospital, how can I direct your call?" "Medical records please." I replied. She transferred my call and corny elevator music could be heard as I waited for a voice to answer on the other end. It felt like forever before anyone answered. I was ready to ask them for my records. My original hospital records. I was ready to see the name and address of the woman who gave birth to me. I felt brave. I felt strong. I felt ready to face the family that deserted me in that hospital 17 years prior. The music stopped and a woman answered, "Medical Records, how can I help you?" I froze. Nothing came out of my mouth. SAY SOMETHING DENISE!!! In panic, I hung up the phone. I stood up, walked around the basement in circles, wiggled my hands free of fear, took some deep breaths and repeated to myself, "You can do this. Call back." So I re-dialed the phone number and was transferred back to Medical Records. This time when the woman answered the phone, I replied, "Hello, My name is Denise Tolbert and I was born at this hospital in 1980. My biological name was Jenise Shacole Carter before I was adopted. I was wondering if you could help me obtain my original hospital documents so that I can identify who gave birth to me." A long pause. "Spell your name for me please," the woman replied. I spelled it for her as I could hear her typing faintly in the background. My heart began to beat faster. "OMG WHAT IF SHE

FINDS WHAT I AM LOOKING FOR," I thought. She sighed deeply and replied, "Honey, I wish I could help you but we are not allowed to release medical records to you until you are 18 years of age. Call back then." "Thanks." I replied and hung up the phone. CALL BACK THEN!!! DO YOU KNOW WHAT IT TOOK FOR ME TO CALL YOU TODAY?!?!?!?! THIS WAS NOT EASY!!! MY ENTIRE LIFE COULD HAVE CHANGED IN ONE MOMENT!!! I felt like a door had been slammed in my face. I let that small barrier defeat me. It took so much courage for me to get to that point on that day, and I got rejected. I went to my room and never talked about searching again for the next eight years.

Yes, 8 years later, I decided to try and reignite my search. I was 25 years old. For some reason, milestone birthdays seemed to be the time in my life that the urge to search crept up on me. I had completed college and graduate school. I was ready. I was older. I was more mature. I was a full adult. My entire outlook on my adoption had changed. As a social worker now, I was more equipped mentally to try this search again. So I pulled out the phone number again and gave my spiel to the woman who answered in Medical Records. "You were born in 1980, correct?" I answered, "Yes, ma'am!" I answered. "I'm sorry to inform you ma'am, but we discard all records after 25 years. We no longer have the requested documents you are looking for." I dropped the phone and walked away. I could hear a faint, "Hello? Hello?" Once again, another door seemed to close in my attempt to find my family. I just wanted a name. Who was it that was at the hospital that gave birth to me? Who signed over any documentation for Jenise Shacole Carter. I went to my room and cried. I cried because I should have just called when I turned 18. I should've just called any time before I turned 25, but I let fear of rejection navigate my attempts.

In 2008, shortly after I had gotten married, I read about a service called "The Locator". I contacted them and a gentleman named Andy asked me for as much information that I had about my biological mother and family members. I began to rattle off the scattered pieces of my history. He told me he would contact me within a week if he found anything. About a week and a half later, he called me back and asked me for some subsequent information to aid with his search. It was information that I did not have, so he informed me that there wasn't much more he could do to help me. He then encouraged me to pursue DNA testing to explore any familial matches. I thanked him and hung up the phone. Why was this so hard? Why couldn't I just send off my DNA to a genetics company to help me find the answers to the questions I had been longing for? Why couldn't anyone just give me what I needed? Fear. The whole idea is just so scary. I just couldn't do it. I was too afraid of what I would find. Also, why wasn't anyone out there looking for me? I hadn't been contacted by anyone looking for their long-lost baby. What if no familial matches could be found? The whole idea wore me out.

I decided from that day on that I would conduct a search of my own by using the internet. I began googling "Jenise Shacole Carter", "Jenise Carter", "Jenise Carter San Diego CA", "Jenise Shacole Carter Twins in California", "Jenise S. Carter inmate/incarceration". I looked up anything and everything I had about myself. Google and Facebook became my investigative team. I began to piece very minimal information together, but nothing concrete ever panned out. Upon one search I stumbled across a Jenise S. Carter who appeared to have been born the same year as my biological mother. The details led me to further identify that this person moved to Fresno, CA but was since deceased. I don't remember the date of death, as I remember immediately putting my cursor on the "close" section of the website tab. I pushed my chair away from the desk and closed my eyes. I didn't cry, but it was the first time that I had actually imagined that the person I had been needing to find my entire life was possibly dead. It had crossed my mind from time to time that my biological mother may not be living. But seeing that birthdate and death date within my search elicited a different feeling. My chest got tight and I remember repeating to myself, "It's probably not even her. It's probably not even her." And it may not be. But the reality of her possibly being deceased hit me in a different way this time. A yearning and a longing for someone to identify with seemed further away than ever before. The questions, the pain, the sadness, the resentment, the need to find out why I was given up to begin with seemed impossible with the mysteriously vague idea that my biological mother is completely unattainable. I got up from my chair and left the office space. I remember going to lay down and just process that entire experience.

In recent years, my mom informed me of a couple of people who still lived in San Diego who may have known my biological mother. Initially I wondered, "Why am I just finding out about these people?" But honestly, I believe that there is a time and season for everything. I may not have been able to handle this information any earlier in my life. There are things that I can accept now as an adult, that 14 year old Denise probably couldn't have handled. My mom ended up giving me the contact information, and I reached out. One of them was allegedly involved in a youth program with my biological mother at the local community center when they were adolescents. I called her but every number I had was disconnected. I didn't feel defeated though. I was very much at peace about where this latest search would go. I had no real expectations about what I would or wouldn't find. The other person I called was the adopted daughter of one of our former church mates from San Diego. She graciously shared her adoption and reunion story with me. Her reunion with her biological mother wasn't exactly a pleasant one in the beginning. When she found her mom, she was explicitly told that she didn't want to be found. Over time their relationship blossomed and she has been in contact with other family members as well. She offered to help me find my family and sent out some messages on social media to see if anyone would respond to her inquiries about the Carter family twin girls. Again, I had no expectations of what would pan out from this. Either I would hear nothing and continue on with my life, or I would get on a plane and fly out to San Diego to meet my biological family. We corresponded a few times about some responses she had received and some info that she had researched. My friend who I had told about this new development asked me, "How do you feel about this? Are you nervous? What if this lady finds your FAMILY?" Throughout the process I was very calm. I wasn't really sure what would come of it. Nothing actually panned out from her attempts to find them, and I wasn't disappointed at all. I wasn't overly elated either when she brought me back possible information. I had a peace about it all. Whatever happened was going to happen. I decided to push pause on this new search for now. I was not upset that I had spent time considering a search again. I was fine. I felt whole. I felt complete. Would it be nice to meet my biological family, of course! But the pain, sadness, and fear of rejection has dissipated. I liked this feeling. Having a family of my own has closed so many of the wounds that kept me bound to a past I had no answers to for so long.

An interesting piece to my adoption story is that I have never once considered looking for my biological father. He honestly never even crossed my mind. Growing up I made up stories about who he was and assumed he probably wasn't in my biological mother's life. I mean he didn't want me or couldn't take me either so he didn't matter to me. Maybe my father was incarcerated as well. Maybe I was a result of a one-night stand. Maybe my biological mom didn't know who my biological dad was. Who knows.

It didn't hit me until recently to look for my biological Aunt.....my biological mother's alleged twin. If my biological mom truly had a twin she is possibly still out there. All of these questions remain and all of these scenarios are still possible. I'm still eager to search and find my identity and complete the circle of wholeness. To truly understand my genetic makeup would be exciting. Sometimes I think about purchasing a plane ticket and flying out to San Diego. For what, I'm not exactly sure. I haven't been back in over twenty years so I have no idea where I am even going. But I feel like I just need to be back in the space. Part of me wants to search for them again. The fear and nervousness about it aren't as strong, as I am much more at peace about where I am in my life. I have healed emotionally from my vague past and endless questions of who I am and where I belong in this world. We shall see what the future holds.

Six
WHO ARE YOU

I remember being of school age and people asking me about my family and my background. I never hesitated to tell people that I was adopted. I often received sad eyes and heavy sighs when I chose to share that with people. Some would respond with "Aww...how do you feel about that?" How do I feel...huh, I'm fine. How do YOU feel. Some other interesting questions or comments that I received from people included:

"You're adopted? Really, but you look just like them."

"What was your orphanage like?"

"THAT was your name? I'm so glad they changed it."

"I wish I was adopted. You're so lucky."

I never really knew quite how to respond to these, they were just a few that really stuck out to me over the years. Nevertheless, I enjoyed sharing that piece of my history with people. I enjoyed answering questions about adoption, and helping people gain a better understanding about what being adopted really meant.

It wasn't until I was a teenager that I really struggled with my identity. I had so many questions that simply couldn't be answered. Questions about who I was, where I came from, and why no one thought I was good enough to keep played like a loop in my head. To me, identity was defined genetically and biologically. It was the foundation of family history but mine was nothing but a mystery. I couldn't connect to anything biologically or genetically, and that was painful. I dealt with that pain for many years by just ignoring it. Sweeping it under the rug and suppressing my feelings about it was how I coped. There was never a space to really talk about it. I didn't really understand what I was even feeling at the time, so trying to articulate these unidentifiable feelings seemed impossible. Adolescent and teen years are the years where individuals seek the most affirmation and seek to establish their status amongst those around them. How could I figure out where I belong amongst my peer group when I didn't even understand my place in this world?

As a teen I always wanted to find somewhere to fit in. I just wanted to belong. I always struggled with feelings of not being enough to people. I felt I had to prove myself in many situations to ensure that people liked me. My self-worth was completely fragmented. I craved attention and constantly avoided confrontation. I just wanted to keep the peace. I had a problem sticking up for myself or asserting myself in certain situations for fear of being rejected and disliked. I never wanted to "rock the boat". The idea that people would be unhappy with me or choose not to be friends with me anymore was devastating. I wasn't going to lose another person in my life. I was going to keep everyone happy and be the silly, goofy, appeasing, loud friend. Drama free and fun loving, that was me. I craved approval from any and everybody. I wanted to feel needed so that I would feel loved. Why? Because how I viewed myself was so poor. My perception of myself was so disjointed from how I presented to people. I'm not sure how I was able to fake it, but I must say I did a great job. No one had a clue that I had such low self-esteem because I aimed to be the life of the party at all times.

I remember having a lot of different sets of friends in high school. Some within what some may call the "popular" crowd, some "artsy" friends, and some that were all about the books. I remember trying to pry my way into different groups to see which one I felt the most accepted in. Which one could I identify with the most. I never got very high grades in high school. I mean they were fine, but I wasn't rocking on the honor roll or anything. I remember being jealous of the girls that seemed to be excelling in their studies and involved in so many extracurricular activities, and even had time for a boyfriend (or two). How did they do it? How did they manage it all? Why did life seem so easy and perfect for them? I was very jealous of the girls that had boyfriends. Why didn't guys want to date me? What was missing from me? What didn't they see in me? I was the bomb!! I was replaying the tapes that I created in my head that told me no one wanted me. So I did what I could to seek attention and go out of my way to try and be seen. I would try and roll my skirts up higher and put on horrific lipstick and lip liner to be something that I wasn't even comfortable being. The only thing I garnered from that was acquiring the title of being "boy crazy". I hated that. I was not that. I simply needed to be validated in some way. I just wanted to be wanted. It was unfair. It's not that I wasn't getting the love from home, but I felt I needed more from my peer group. What was wrong with me? Why wasn't I happy just being me? I wonder if my biological mom was the same way in this aspect of my personality. Was my sole desire to gain the approval and love from others because SHE gave me away and I wasn't good enough to keep? Yea, that must be it. I allowed myself to believe that. It was all her fault. All of it. If she had just kept me none of this would be happening.

I was never one to get in trouble in high school. I was always afraid of getting grounded or embarrassing my parents. I never got detention, or suspended, or skipped school. I was always too afraid of the repercussions. I remember one day a group of my friends skipped class to take the bus down to what was once known as City Place Mall in Silver Spring, Maryland. They asked me to go, but I was way too afraid. What if our parents found out? What if we got expelled? My mind always went to the extreme. Well, they went and ended up coming back with tattoos. No one ever found out and to this day I wish I went and wasn't such a chicken, but I was. One of my classmates who was adopted as well told me one day, "I avoid trouble with my adoptive parents because somewhere in the back of my mind I'm afraid they will find a way to give me back. To whom? I don't know. But I stay clear of their disapproval." Whew! That thought never even entered my mind. How awful it must be to try and be the "perfect child" in fear of being relinquished all over again.

By the 11th grade, I realized I no longer really cared what people thought of me. I decided I was going to just be me, whoever that was. I wanted to stop trying to be something I wasn't and gain approval from people who didn't really matter. With this new-found nonchalance, I decided to try new things. I remember going through a short lived goth apparel period and shaving the back of my head to about the tip of my earlobe. I was briefly enamored with everything 70's- lava lamps, black light, incense, and mod clothing. Then began my desire to experiment with cigarettes. I remember a couple of my friends decided that they were going to start smoking cigarettes as well. Some of my schoolmates would sneak across the street from school to the neighboring 7-Eleven and buy packs of them. I'm not sure how they were able to purchase them, but they did and they would bring cartons back. I remember being offered a cigarette behind the gymnasium at my high school and holding it in my hand. I remember thinking, "I wonder if my biological mother smoked cigarettes?" "I wonder what age she started smoking and abusing drugs?" "Who gave them to her?" I placed the cigarette to my lips, leaned my head forward and graciously accepted the light that had been offered to me. I took a long, slow drag as the smoke entered my body. I remember coughing uncontrollably. It burned. The back of my throat felt like it was on fire. It literally hurt my chest, but I pretended to be a pro and delicately flicked the ashes on the pavement. I put the cigarette to my mouth again and continued until I got to the butt of it. I would spray myself with Pear Glace' body splash from Victoria's Secret, and would fill my mouth with Binaca Peppermint Breath Spray so that my secret wouldn't get out. I'm not sure how I kept it from so many people, but I did. From that day forward I found creative ways to obtain my own cigarette packs, and found myself smoking alone often. I usually only smoked 2 cigarettes a day, so I always had packs for months at a time. I always wondered why people got addicted to cigarettes. I didn't understand what the attraction was. Why did it seem to ease people's moods and remove the stresses of everyday life? It literally did nothing for me. Maybe because I wasn't smoking on a regular. My body never craved them.

I never seemed to get addicted, which was my goal. As bizarre as it sounds, I was looking for something to get addicted to. My biological mother had addiction issues and for some reason I was so desperate for a connection with her. I wanted something to have in common with her whether it was negative or positive. I never verbalized this to anyone because it sounds utterly ridiculous. I simply wanted to feel what it was like to want and need something so bad. I wanted to understand why and how it was impossible to give up. My mother didn't give it up. She continued to abuse drugs. Drugs that remained in me as she left me at the hospital and went on with her life.

I wanted her to fight for me. I wanted to be something worth fighting for. But I wasn't. She still left me. For six months I miserably failed at addicting myself to nicotine. I remember sitting at the park behind my parents' house with a cigarette hanging from my mouth and looking at the rest in the pack. Lauryn Hill's song "Ex-Factor" played in my cd-man as I shook my head and decided right then and there that I was going to quit smoking. For one, my attempts to get hooked were not working, and secondly, the latest campaign ads for www.truth.com were guilting me into the dangers of nicotine and the many reasons to stop. I took that half full packet, broke all of the cigarettes in half and dumped them in the trash. I am extremely grateful that I did not spiral into a life of addiction and move to alcohol and drugs. The desire to connect was stronger than any rationale that suggested that what I was doing was quite self-destructive. I am thankful that these maladaptive behaviors never stuck.

In college, I experienced my first significant relationship. It lasted several years, but eventually we went our separate ways. I believe my fear of not being enough for him allowed me to decide that it was time to call it quits. My mistrust of people and fear of them leaving me before I could leave them stuck with me through most of my romantic relationships. I would break up with you before you could break up with me.

They weren't going to get rid of me. I was getting rid of them. I was direly afraid of losing relationships. I was afraid of losing people. I was afraid of losing love. I was always afraid that I wasn't enough for the people in my life and I couldn't offer them what they needed. However, no one was going to discard me again. It all stemmed back to being adopted, and I never realized exactly what I was doing. Erasing people before they could erase me. I believed that allowing myself to get close to members of the opposite sex opened me up to getting deserted. I had an incessant fear of being rejected and abandoned. This fear glared through most of my relationships.

When I think back to what I could've been brought up in, I am more than grateful. Let me be explicitly clear. I am undeniably thankful for being adopted. I wouldn't trade the life God afforded me for anything else in this world. But something was missing. Something has always been missing. There was never a time that I didn't feel that. It became more apparent the older I got. As I began to form more meaningful relationships, I began to conceptualize the idea of being adopted. There was never a space or a time to explore these feelings that I had; the feelings of void of my identity, emptiness, abandonment, feeling disconnected, and issues of self-worth. I honestly don't believe either of my parents knew these types of conversations were necessary. I don't know if they knew how to facilitate that conversation. I surely didn't. It definitely wouldn't have been a one-time thing. It would have taken several discussions to embark on the lifelong journey of being an adoptee. Being a teen is kind of a time period between "I want be left alone but don't leave me alone". Would I have even WANTED to talk to them about all of this if they tried? How could I explain to them that I was so sad sometimes or that I felt so alone? How was I going to describe that I was grieving the loss of my name and a mother that chose to give me away? I mean it's pretty strange how much you can miss someone you have never met. How would they understand that? Because I sure didn't. I just tried to silence the thoughts that I had and reminded myself that I simply needed to be thankful that I was adopted.

I remember attempting to have conversations with some friends about being adopted and some of my feelings about it. Thinking back, some of their reactions were atrocious. Needless to say, they are no longer my friends. I remember one telling me, "You should just be happy you got a good family." Ummmm I don't remember saying I wasn't happy, I was simply emoting. Guess that was the wrong one to vent to. Another person expressed to me, "I don't understand why you feel that way. It could've been much worse." Well, yes my adoption could have been a horrific experience, but I just needed a listening ear at that point. Someone else had the gall to say, "You can't be mad at your mom and her choice. She made it, and you got the great end of the deal." Deal? *DEAL?* I always thought that a deal was defined as a mutual agreement between two people. I guarantee I wasn't a part of that decision. No deals were made with me on her decision. I promise it wouldn't have been mutual. People mean well but they just don't know what to say sometimes. My adoption experience was MY experience and since no one seemed to understand it, I bottled up my feelings about the whole thing.

My dad and I had several conversations about my adoption as I began writing this book. He informed me that before a child is adopted, all family members of the child on both the maternal and paternal side are contacted first. This allows them the opportunity to decide if they are able to take the child and provide care to the child before it is placed in the foster care system. Apparently none of them jumped at this opportunity. Nobody. For whatever reason, nobody wanted me. In 37 years of my life that was my first time hearing that part of my story. My entire heart sank into my stomach. I was rejected by an entire family? That was heavy. Was there NO ONE that thought they could do what was done for my sister Erin? Not a grandmother, an aunt, not even a cousin. No one. I wasn't mad when I found this out. I was more disappointed and stunned. I was unaware of that protocol so to hear that hurt. I won't lie, I wept. Not because no one stepped up and took me, but because apparently no one could. I can only imagine the generational turmoil and chaos that I could have been brought up in. So again, I began to give thanks that *they chose me* to let go of.

JENISE AT 11 MONTHS (1981) IN HER FOSTER HOME

AN ADOPTION STORY

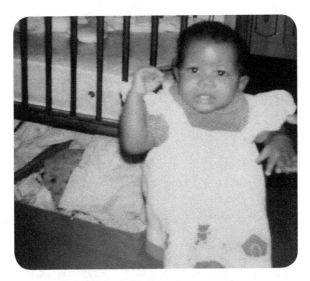

JENISE AGE 1 IN HER FOSTER HOME(1981)

BABY JENISE- 14 MONTHS IN FOSTER CARE (1982)

JENISE AT 14 MOS WITH HER FOSTER MOTHER

JENISE ON A VISIT WITH TOLBERT FAMILY EXPLORING THEIR
HOME (1981)

JENISE AND FRANCES (1981)

JENISE MEETING HER GRANDPARENTS AARON
AND MABEL JONES (1981)

A VISIT TO THE TOLBERT HOME (1982)

FAMILY PICTURES (1982)

FIRST FAMILY PORTRAIT (1982)

AN ADOPTION STORY

ALL SMILES (1982)

JENISE AT 16 MOS AT THE TOLBERT'S HOME (1982)

BIRTHDAY CELEBRATIONS (1982)

ADOPTION DAY- JULY 8,1983

DENISE AGE 8 VISITING FAMILY IN ROCHESTER, NY (1989)

SISTERS: ERIN AND DENISE (2010)

WEDDING DAY (2008)
Photo Credit: Shades of Gray Photography

DAVID AND DENISE (2010)

PROUD PARENTS AWAITING DAYNA'S ARRIVAL (2011)
Photo Credit: ScroleVision Photography

DAYNA AT 5 DAYS OLD (2011)

DEFOE HOLIDAY FAMILY PHOTO SHOOT (2016)
Photo Credit: Elroy B. Photograhy

DENISE WITH HER PARENTS AND DAUGHTER, DAYNA.
(2015)

Seven

THE SHIFT

For many years I resented my biological mother for her decision to give me up. How could she do such a thing? I was her child. I struggled with so much anger, grief, and confusion for so long. It was hard to shake. It wasn't something that I could ignore, no matter how hard I tried. I didn't talk about it much, but it was there..... bubbling up. It wasn't until college that my perspective on my adoption completely changed.

I began my Freshman year at Oakwood College (now University) in the Fall of 1999. I started out as Psychology major and after one semester, I changed my major to Social Work. We were assigned a 15-20 page paper called the "Introspection Assignment" during our Junior year. This assignment required us to take a reflective look at our lives and explore events that had shaped us into the people that we had become up until that point in our lives. I thought long and hard to identify any significant and or influential events over the past 21 years of my life. I really couldn't think of anything and then it hit me. My adoption. I began to seriously think about what it meant to me to be adopted and assessed my feelings that went along with it. As I sat at the computer at my desk in Wade Hall, the feelings began to swell. My emotions erupted like a hot molten volcano. Every feeling that I had ever felt exploded. The anger about how someone could disrupt such a genuinely emotional bond turned into feelings of worthlessness and despair. I began dwelling on my feelings around the need to obtain approval from others because the one person who should've seen the value in me gave me away. The feelings of emptiness and confusion overtook me. For years I would yell and cry about how selfish she was for not trying, for not choosing me, for not giving up habits and lifestyles that would prevent her from being what I needed – my mother. The resentment for a woman I didn't even know overpowered me at that desk. The grief of losing the one person who should have wanted me the most, drowned my heart with sorrow and heartache. The thought that I had no sense of being for 21 years simply because she didn't fight for me, enraged me.

With tears in my eyes, I placed my hands on the keyboard and began to type. I started writing about the pain and the agony I felt and the longing I had to feel like I belonged. As I was typing, my attitude about being adopted began to immediately shift with each keystroke. The perspective that I had about my mom was all wrong. She wasn't selfish. What she did was the bravest thing she could have ever done. She gave me a chance. She could have terminated her pregnancy with me, but she didn't. She made the decision to keep me and allow me to have a life that she knew she couldn't provide. It was probably the hardest choice she had ever had to make. I couldn't imagine what she went through.

I began to think long and hard about why I was so angry with her after being given such an amazing life. I had been given the opportunity to attend college, meet amazing friends and mentors, and experience unconditional love by two people who chose me to be a part of their family. In that moment, the wording in my paper began to change, my emotions began to change, and my facial expression started to change. Right then and there it hit me like a ton of bricks; my adoption was the biggest blessing in my life.

The choice that my biological mother made required a sacrifice from her. It required her to decide in her mind to say goodbye to me forever. Her decision shifted my life's narrative. I was no longer mad at her, I was thankful to her.

I was thankful that she didn't subject me to years of drug and alcohol abuse and who knows what else.

I was thankful I did not have to endure years of men in and out of her life and possible financial hardship.

I was thankful for the opportunity to finish high school and continue on to higher education.

I was thankful that she allowed me the opportunity to break some generational curses, and avoid some of the pitfalls that may have impeded her life.

I still didn't have all the answers to my many questions, nor did I fully understand what made everything click that day, but it did. For that I am thankful. I do not have any ill feelings toward my biological mother anymore. Through this assignment, I was able to fully examine feelings and behaviors that I had experienced growing up. I was able to conceptualize something I didn't think I ever would. In that moment, I chose forgiveness. I chose to forgive my biological mother for the decision that she made. A decision that kept me filled with resentment, anger and sadness. I released myself of the weight of anguish. I freed my mother from the bounds of my disdain towards her. It was a complicated journey to get here still with unanswered questions, but I committed to the journey to dismiss a grudge towards someone I didn't know and who didn't know a grudge had been established. The selfless act of adoption allowed me to recognize how thankful I was that my parents chose me to take me into their home and give me the best life I could have ever imagined. I was given a family who surrounded me with unconditional love and support.

My biological mother selflessly chose to give me up. It was a viewpoint that I had to shift within my mind. I had always associated her decision as a selfish one. One that didn't take much thought or consideration. I believed that she chose her life over me. However, by allowing myself to change the narrative I recognized that in making her decision she did in fact consider me. She chose to give me a chance. She gave me an opportunity to have a new start. I am living within my purpose thanks to that class assignment. I must say college was a four-year "Aha" moment.

Eight

CAN YOU TELL ME ABOUT YOUR MEDICAL HISTORY

"Can you tell me about your medical history," the nurse says to me eager to complete her medical intake forms. "No. I cannot," I respond. That is the extent of my answer with an elaborate eye roll every time I'm asked this question by a medical professional. Of course it's not their fault that I don't know my medical history, and yes I know it's simply a standard question asked for medical intake. However, being asked this question elicited a reaction that is equivalent to someone scratching their fingernails on a chalkboard. It frustrated me drawing lines through boxes labeled "unknown". It made me feel like an alien in my own body. I literally don't know. For a while, I would just snarkily draw a line through the forms and scribble in large letters ADOPTED: HISTORY UNKNOWN. It is an extremely scary feeling not knowing ANYTHING about my family medical history. Did my loved ones have a history of cancer? Dementia? Mental Illness? Infertility? Congenital diseases? It is unnerving at times to just not know. I don't think about it much anymore because I've been relatively healthy. However, from time to time it crosses my mind.

In July of 2008, three months before my wedding, I went to the doctor after discovering a lump in my left breast. The first question the doctor asked me was, "Does anyone in your family have a history of lumpy breasts or breast cancer?" With tears in my eyes I responded, "I sure wish I could tell you." I wished I could say, "You know what, yes! My mom and grandma both have been told that they have lumpy breasts but it's never been cancerous, that's probably what it is." I wished desperately that I could say that because I FEARED that this lump sitting on my breast in all its firmness was cancer, and the man that I had prayed, for who asked me to be his wife, was going to have to care for a cancer patient and possibly be a widow within a year of marrying me. I was terrified. My fiancé came with me to the next doctor's appointment. We sat in silence patiently waiting for the scan results which revealed nothing but fatty tissue. We rejoiced at the good news, but that incident incited a fear in me that I had never felt before.

Many adoptees struggle with this. The desire to know. We have a hunger to know what our past may mean for our future. Not having access to that information leaves you hanging in the balance and somewhat blind to the preventative practice of medicine. My original medical records have been disposed of, but many states have passed legislation that grant access to adoptees interested in obtaining that information.

Genetic testing has come a long way over the years and we are able to obtain information that was not attainable 20 years ago. These tests are able to fill in so many gaps that create so much uneasiness and uncertainty in the mind of the adoptee. They can be a dynamic tool to give individuals more information and make more informed decisions. Many people have asked me why I haven't done genetic testing. Part of me probably doesn't really want to know. With all of the advancements in medical testing and genetic research and as helpful as the information would be, it can also be nerve-wracking. Today there are many websites that offer individuals the opportunity to send off a urine, saliva, or blood sample to their corporation and within a matter of a week, you will obtain an array of results that reveal what medical conditions are prevalent in your family. Having the information would be nice, but wouldn't necessarily prevent me or my child from getting something. It would also invoke a minor case of hypochondriasis, which also isn't beneficial. Who knows, at some point I may reach out and look into it further. For now I am ok not knowing. However, if having this information is important to you, get it while you can. Knowing your medical history can save your life.

Nine
FINDING LOVE

I met my husband David in May of 2007. We were introduced by a mutual friend at a church group meeting for young adults. I didn't realize he was a Pastor and I was actually shocked to find that out. He was so "real". He didn't seem to be pretentious; he was so down to earth. At the end of the meeting I very innocently and without intent asked our mutual friend if David was married. A huge grin came upon our friend's face and he responded, "I got you." I rolled my eyes, chuckled, and walked away. Two weeks later we shared dinner at this same friend's home, went on our first date, and were engaged 10 months later. It was truly love at first.....conversation. At the time, both of us had gotten out of pretty serious relationships and I had actually given up on love. I was tired of dating random people. I believed God was going to send me who He had for me. And He did.

Being a Pastor, David had a pretty hectic schedule and at times, I felt like he was avoiding me. He probably wasn't, but I again was allowing those feelings of fear and abandonment to creep in and sabotage a relationship that I was pretty sure was going to be my last. Thoughts like, "maybe he doesn't think I'll be a good Pastor's wife", "maybe I'm not wife material", or "I'll never be enough for him", crept in immediately. But I knew from our first date that we were going to be married, so why did I feel like he was trying to play me? I wasn't going to let the man I prayed for get rid of me. I decided I'll fix him. I remember telling my best friend how I was feeling about the relationship. She advised me to go over his house and be open with him about how I was feeling about the relationship. Forget that, I was going over there to DUMP him. I wasn't going to allow him to try and distance himself from me. I refused to end up hearing him request a sorrowful sit down conversation with me beginning with "We are just growing apart" or "It's not you, it's me". NOPE! I remember calling him sternly to let him know we needed to talk and that I was on my way over. I had my speech prepared, well written out in my notes section on my phone. I had rehearsed what I was going to say; hopefully without tears. I wanted him to know I was serious and was not backing down from my decision. I remember starting my dialogue and he snarkily interrupted me as if to say by my tone that he knew what this visit was going to be about. His voice sarcastically told me, "Just stop. You're not breaking up with me. You know I love you and I'm not going anywhere". I was so stunned, and a little upset that I didn't get to share my carefully crafted script with him, but his reassurance within that moment felt permanent. A feeling that I hadn't felt before. In that moment I was able to let go of past hurts, failed relationships, and fear of not being loved. His words were genuine. They secured my feelings that in fact we would be together forever.

Allowing myself to be loved took time and work within myself. I had to cast out my fears of being abandoned and push aside the echoing thoughts of low self-esteem and feelings of not being wanted. I had to allow myself to believe that I was capable and deserving of a stable and loving relationship. Fully relinquishing the fear of instability and discord helped shape my platonic and romantic relationships. I had to reconcile within myself that I was worthy of love and protection. All of the things David longed to give me. Our relationship helped me fully understand how I give love and how I need to receive it. We have been married now for ten glorious years, and are proud parents to our sweet daughter, Dayna. Every day isn't filled with rainbows and unicorns but I can honestly say that processing my fears of being in relationships and allowing myself to be loved was the best work within myself that I have done. It is a journey, one worth taking. My husband has been supportive of my adoption healing journey and fully understands my needs and insecurities, and has loved me through it all.

Ten

BECOMING MOMMY

On January 8, 2011 I found out I was pregnant. I wept with joy and remember screaming to David that we were having a baby. In disbelief, we hugged and began calling our family and closest friends. It was a very emotional moment. One that I will never forget.

For me pregnancy had a very special meaning. Not only was I a human incubator for God's greatest gifts, but I finally had a connection with someone who had my blood running through their veins. The little 6-week embryo inside of my body shared my DNA. I was finally going to meet someone that I was biologically related to. That was huge to me. Yea, pregnancy was DEEP for me. I cherished this responsibility. I was going to do everything I could to ensure that I took care of my body and that my baby was healthy. My baby was going to know that this mommy wasn't going anywhere.

Pregnancy is truly a 40-week faith walk. I was so nervous. I prayed so hard that God would bless my baby and keep my body strong during that time. I talked and read and sang to my belly every day. I loved every minute of pregnancy, until the end when I had to sleep sitting up. I relished every kick, squirm, nudge, and flip. My husband can't say I was a crazy pregnant lady; well he can but it wouldn't be true. I was 30 when I found out I was pregnant so the doctors monitored me a bit closer due to my age {insert eye roll} and my history of fibroids that I learned of at my first OBGYN appointment. At six weeks pregnant, David and I went to our first prenatal appointment to hear the baby's heartbeat. I remember my Obstetrician picking up a bottle of Aquasonic sonogram gel and squeezing a fistful across my belly. She then took the ultrasound probe and smeared the warming jelly across my navel. A small peanut shaped figure appeared on the black and white screen of the sonography machine. It was the first look at our baby. The doctor turned on the sound and the strongest little heartbeat erupted through the speaker. We remember the doctor leaning into the screen a little closer and staring for a second. She turned and looked at us and exclaimed, "It looks like it might be twins!!" I leapt up and screamed, "WHAT!?!" The initial thought that I may be having twins was so exciting. Always hearing that my biological mother may have been a twin and now I may be having them made my entire day. I was completely amped. I have heard that twins "skip" a generation. I'm not sure how accurate that is, but my birth certificate identifies that I was a singleton birth.

David on the other hand was in a bit of shock and disbelief. I believe his initial response was, "Oh My God!" The OB began to press harder on my belly to listen for that second heartbeat that wasn't there. From there she surmised that what was once my baby's identical twin (in my head) was actually a fibroid of the same size as my embryo. Womp. I began dismissing cute twin names from my head. The thought was fun for those seven minutes though.

She went on to explain that I would be monitored relatively closely with an increased number of sonograms to ensure that the fibroids discovered would not grow too rapidly with the baby and block my birth canal. More sonograms were just fine with me. I enjoyed catching a glimpse of my little baby and seeing the little fetus growing and developing on that screen. I wished I knew if any of the women in my family had fibroids. Did any of them have difficult pregnancies? I wasn't going to allow my mind to worry. The fibroids thankfully didn't cause any problems during my pregnancy. They occasionally created interesting shapes to my growing belly when the baby would stretch, but that is all.

There were also a series of genetic tests done to rule out any genetic disorders at around thirteen weeks. I remember being extremely nervous as the testing date approached. The scan begun and several measurements, probes and pictures taken. A week later, the physician from the fetal testing center called me back in and explained to me that my baby had an echogenic intracardiac focus on its heart. An echogenic focus is a small "bright spot" on the heart that can be seen during an ultrasound. It was one of many markers for Down's Syndrome. I remember getting extremely hot. I began to sweat and the words coming out of her mouth no longer made sense. Did my baby have Downs? Would more "markers" show up? Were there children in my biological family that had Downs? This is all my fault. I should've done genetic testing sooner? Will all of my children have this? The next words that came out of the doctor's mouth were, "Your baby is not showing any other markers, just this small illuminated spot on its heart that is likely a calcium deposit. It is not a heart defect, and it likely will not have Down's Syndrome. I am just obligated to tell you what I see." As I exhaled deeply, my worries and fears went away. Blame and guilt for not knowing my genetic makeup subsided. I prayed that little marker would magically disappear. It did not, but that's ok.

In my nineteenth week of pregnancy we found out the gender of our baby. It was a girl! We were elated. Dayna Imara Defoe was the name that we chose for her. As soon as we left the doctor's office we headed to the mall to buy as many dresses and baby girl merchandise that you could possibly imagine. As we walked the mall, I began to wonder if my biological mother found out my gender before I was born. I wondered if she was even excited to be pregnant with me or if I was nothing more than a mistake. Did she even care? I loved going to the OBGYN; did she dread it? Was I a constant reminder to her of a choice she wish she didn't make? At times I wondered why she didn't terminate her pregnancy with me if she already knew she was just going to give me a way. I'm glad she went through with the pregnancy.

At around week 31 in my pregnancy, I went in for another scheduled sonogram with my husband. As the sonographer proceeded with the exam, a look of confusion came across her face. I asked her what was wrong. She simply grinned and exited the room. I remember poking my belly really hard to elicit a response from Dayna just to make sure she would move; boy did she kick me back. The sonographer returned with the Fetal specialist who looked over the screen and nodded as the sonographer pointed at what just looked like specks of nothingness to me. She turned and looked at me and asked me, "Mrs.

Defoe, have you ever been pregnant before?" I responded no, just as my paperwork indicated. She then asked me, "Are you sure? Your placenta looks older than it is as if this is not your first". I sat up angrily as this woman insinuated in front of my husband that I was unsure if I had carried life before and may have simply forgot that small detail. I gave her a remarkably stank face and sternly assured her that I was positive and to continue on with the exam. I asked her if everything was ok with my baby and she said it was. I never thought more about that conversation until week thirty-seven.

It was my final scheduled sonogram and kind of a bittersweet moment. I knew that in about 2-3 weeks my baby would be here, but I really enjoyed the process of getting sonograms. The sonographer and fetal specialist entered the room to inform me that Dayna looked to be only weighing in at around 3 lbs 14 oz. They had concerns that she wouldn't gain much more weight in the next 3 weeks and that it was best to take her out. It was the scariest feeling I had ever felt in my life. I felt helpless. I kept thinking "She's not ready. I'm not ready. I still had 3 weeks left!!!!"

They left the room and made some phone calls to the hospital and faxed over several papers to them. They contacted my OBGYN to inform her of their plan and she was in agreement with an induction in two days. TWO DAYS?!?!? I was taken to a back room with about 4 hospital beds and monitors to complete my stress test. It was dimly lit and there was one other lady back there getting one done for her baby. They strapped my belly to a machine and turned on a bunch of monitors. I remember texting my husband and our families to give them an update as to why my appointment which was usually about 30 minutes was dragging onto an hour and a half. I remember feeling like I was going to faint. Anxiety took over. I forced myself to breathe deeply and relax so I wouldn't stress myself into labor at that moment. With tears in my eyes, I laid back on the hospital bed and began to pray for my baby. I prayed that Dayna would be ok during labor and delivery. There was nothing else I could do. Nothing. A tech came back and presented me with a letter to give to my employer to inform them that I would need to be on bedrest for the next two days until my induction. She saw that I had been crying and assured me that everything would be ok. She told me to turn in my letter and get excited that I would be bringing home a baby that weekend. I am pretty sure that I was still in shock and definitely not as excited as she was.

I went home that evening and began to process the whole afternoon. I needed to wrap my mind around the fact that my baby was very tiny and would be born in just a few days. It was a lot. Would Dayna need the neonatal intensive care unit? Would there be complications? Will I physically be ok? Would I need a C-section? I didn't plan for that!!!! What was the rush? Why couldn't we just wait a little longer? At that moment I began to again wonder about my biological family. Did my mother have any complications with her pregnancies? Did any of the women in my family experience preterm labor? Did my grandmother have fibroids? Were Carter babies born small? Did this run in our family? HOW was I supposed to know these things!! There was no one to pre-warn me of this. I was so frustrated and angry and sad at the same time. Why is this happening to me? There was nothing I could do to change any of this, but my mind always wandered back to my biological family when things went "wrong" in my life. I suppose I was looking for someone to blame.

I was induced and on August 19, 2011 weighing in at a whopping 4lbs 8oz, Dayna was born. She was perfectly healthy and did not have to go to the NICU. After delivery, it was discovered that I had a placental infarction. This happens when there is an interruption in blood flow between the placenta and the baby. Basically my placenta died and Dayna was not receiving any more nutrients or anything from me. Apparently mine was pretty large and if I had waited any longer to deliver, Dayna would have been stillborn. However, God stepped in. I am so thankful for those fibroids. If I did not have them, I would not have been monitored so closely.

Three days after giving birth I was discharged from the hospital. There was a feeling of relief and fear. I was relieved that my labor and delivery went well and we both were healthy. I was afraid because I was somebody's mother! She was so tiny. I was afraid I would break her. I remember being wheeled out of my hospital room after completing all of the discharge paperwork. Dayna and I waited in the lobby of the hospital while David went to go pull the car around so that our family of three could head home. It was a rainy Sunday and I sat with Dayna in her infant carrier on my lap as we waited. I remember my eyes filled with tears. I was already extremely emotional from giving birth- darn hormones. These tears were different...I began to think about my birth mother. How could she leave the hospital without me? I remember clutching Dayna's carrier closer to me as I continued to weep. I wondered who came and picked up my biological mother from the hospital? What was that car ride like for her? Did ANYONE try and make her change her mind? Did the discharge planners and hospital staff make SURE she wanted to leave me there? Did she have any visitors see us? Did they say anything? Did she ever come back to the nursery to see me? Did she go back to jail upon discharge? So many questions. So much pain. I couldn't imagine leaving without me. But she did, and I am thankful for her decision. I have no idea the life she returned to when she left me there at University Hospital. Whatever it was couldn't accommodate me. It wasn't a conducive enough environment for my biological mother to adequately meet my needs. She knew that. I wonder if her family and friends understood that. I wonder where my biological father was in all of this? Did he have a say? Did he know I existed? Did he even care?

What I did know was that I was going to be the best mother I could to my new baby. For 37 weeks Dayna and I shared a bond like none other. While in utero we connected biologically, genetically, psychologically, and spiritually. She heard my heartbeat. She felt my emotions through chemical signals and responded to my touch. She heard my voice and the voice of her father and other family and friends who are a part of her life. That bond is one that I will never forget. It was surreal to know that I carried the only family member that I'll possibly ever know that shares my DNA.

For me that bond was broken postnatally. For 40 weeks my biological mother and I shared this same bond and it was severed after I was born. After my birth I remained in the hospital for 28 days while strangers attended to me. I was left alone with no biological or genetic proxy to come care for me or show me love. I had no one to console my cries, no one to sing me to sleep, no one to assure me that they loved me and that they would do anything for me. Hospital staff. Nurses doing rounds. Caring people I'm sure, but that's who I was left with. I was a boarder baby. By definition I was an infant who stayed in the nursery after the mother's discharge. Were there volunteers who came to see me to provide "cuddle care" since I was born addicted to drugs? How awful.

To this day Dayna and I are extremely close. I take sheer pride in being her mother and I cherish our relationship. People joke with me about how much I LOVE Dayna. They say it's amazing how much I dote on her and how she is definitely my favorite person on the planet, after David of course. I assumed all moms share this sentiment, but apparently, I can be a bit over the top. I'll own that. I confess that I'm a smidge overly affectionate and protective of her. Well she is my only child and I can admit that I overcompensate a bit because of the maternal bond I lost as an infant. I just want her to know and understand that her mother's love is unconditional and unwavering. I do hope it doesn't impede her ability to be resilient and independent. I want her to be able lead and love and assert herself with respect and confidence. I believe I have found a balance in coddling and promoting self-sufficiency.

Being a mom has completely changed who I am as a person. There is a sense of wholeness. I have what I have been seeking my entire life. Connection. Biological attachment. I finally found someone who looks like me, sounds like me, has a personality like me. I gush when people remark, "Dayna looks just like you." or "Dayna definitely has your personality". My whole life I had no one to which those attributes applied to. But now I do and it means the entire world to me.

Dayna is a piece of me. She will never fully understand how deep my love for her is. She will know that I take motherhood extremely seriously. It is a responsibility that was given to me that I am fully invested in. There is nothing I wouldn't do for that child. She will unequivocally know that I will always be here for her. I will never judge her for the decisions she makes or the person that she becomes. I will forever be proud of her and will allow her to unashamedly be herself. I'm not naïve, I know that there will be periods of time that we will not get along. That comes along with the teen tide, but I know we will always be close. She has my entire heart and I have vowed to be the mom my biological mother couldn't be for me.

Eleven
WHOLE

I remember preparing to write this book and talking with David pretty openly about my adoption around my then 6 year old daughter, Dayna. I was simply getting more details and ensuring that I had all of the documents that I needed to accurately tell my story. I didn't actually realize that Dayna didn't know I was adopted. It never really came up. I had always planned to tell her. When? I don't know. I wasn't hiding it from her, I was just waiting for a time to talk with her about it with understanding. I think she knew that her "Mimi", my mom didn't carry me in her tummy, but I don't think she truly understood what it meant to be adopted. One evening David and I were talking about the book, and Dayna in her precocious voice said, "Mommy, you were adopted? Your mommy didn't want you?" I froze. My husband found it opportune to walk into another room and I was left to answer this pretty difficult question. I responded, "No, my mommy couldn't take care of me, so Mimi adopted me." She likened my adoption to that of the movie "Annie" and wondered if my foster mom was mean like Miss Hannigan in the film. I assured her she wasn't. I continued on with a fairly age appropriate explanation about adoption and what all is involved. She was intrigued by what I had to say.

Dayna is a very contemplative child. She didn't say much after that conversation. About three days later, she climbed into my bed and nuzzled into my bosom. She held me very tight and looked into my eyes. What she said next was astonishing. "Mommy, I'm glad your mommy gave you to Mimi. If she didn't you wouldn't have gotten taken care of and you wouldn't be my mommy. You are the best mommy ever." Tears filled my eyes and I wept. I hugged that little girl so tight and told her she was exactly right. I went to my room to retrieve my adoption albums. I showed her pictures and explained details about my adoption. She was really engaged and liked learning more about that piece of me. It felt good telling her. I will continue to talk with her about it openly if she has more questions.

The year 2017 was a pretty rough year for me emotionally. A lot of emptiness as it related to my career and lifelong goals took over my outlook on life. A lot of it had to do with a new medication I was on as a means of birth control. Every month I would experience about two to three days of deep depression. I have never had issues with clinical depression, so I knew that what I was feeling wasn't right. It was almost an out of body experience. I felt like I was looking inside of a bubble at my depressed self. I was fully aware of how I felt and I hated it. I remember thinking to myself, "People feel like this every single day of their life?" I was in disbelief of how sad I felt. I would tell myself, "This will only last a few days. It always does. Just push through, you will be fine." The days were filled with darkness and despair, hopelessness and worthlessness. And then poof they were gone. Knowing that the birth control was accurately working was enough for me to continue using it. I remember in the spring getting a bit more tearful and reclusive. I was losing my light. I contemplated ending my life. No, I didn't have a plan and no, I never told anyone. I just dealt with it internally and pushed through the feelings of anguish. I remember telling myself, "I wonder if anyone would even miss me if I were to die besides Dayna. I don't do anything meaningful. I haven't accomplished much. Would people even really care? Really? They probably would all just feel bad and come to my funeral because I'm Pastor Defoe's wife?" I couldn't believe I thought this, it consumed me. I remember these pockets of sadness regularly throughout the year. People around me seemed to be attaining so much and I felt so small. Friends were getting new jobs and starting businesses. Some were writing books and re-enrolling into school. I kept feeling so mediocre. I felt like a loser. I felt like I had nothing to contribute to the world and my family would be embarrassed by my nothingness. I had no new goals, no new aspirations. I just felt like a nobody. My husband has a bountiful love for learning and working. He pursues them like a drug addict seeks drugs. He thrives from learning and works very hard. The idea of being able to provide for his family is extremely moving to watch. So, I began to question myself. Does he see me as lazy? Do I come off as someone with no drive? Am I just a wife and mother to him? Does he view me as visionless, and not living within my purpose? I sat him down one evening and had this conversation with him and he sadly couldn't understand how I could even formulate those questions in my head. He reassured me that what I was thinking was erroneous, and we talked through my feelings. After a discussion with my primary care physician, I made the decision to stop the medication. My physician felt this option was best for me. Within a few weeks I was feeling back to my regular self. No more periods of sadness, worthlessness, or hopelessness. No more negative views on who I was or where I was supposed to be in my life. I often wonder if my biological mother or anyone in my biological family dealt with anxiety or depression. I wondered if anyone in my family suffered from mental illness. It was quite a scary time that I never want to experience again.

Looking back over my life I can identify situations that I purposefully avoided because I was too anxious or nervous to fail, so I wouldn't even try. I remember in high school wanting to run for student office but being too afraid that no one would vote for me and that I wouldn't be what they needed in a leader. I knew I was fully capable of campaigning and even holding the office, but I allowed my fears and anxiety to derail some of my own ambitions. The fear of not being enough and disapproval would creep in during those situations. I firmly believe that everyone has some fear of failure. It's always a bit nerve wracking to try something new and be unsure of how people will receive it. For adoptees however, I believe there is another layer to this. A layer that travels back to the day that the child was taken from the mother and given up for adoption. Not feeling valued or needed by the person who relinquished us follows us throughout our entire adoption journey. This fear and anxiety is a constant reminder of being abandoned and rejected by the people that should have loved us the most.

In 2018 I visited one of my closest friends, Carmen, in Winston Salem, NC with a few of my girlfriends to bring in the New Year. We had a wonderful weekend of relaxation, sisterhood, and retreat. It was a time to get a break from work, our children, and just everyday life. Carmen's mom, Beverly, affectionately known as Auntie Bev, came over to her home to say hi to us. Every person she comes in contact with leaves her presence feeling filled and empowered. She makes you feel like you can conquer the world! She sat and asked us about goals for the new year and what our ambitions were. She spoke with us about the importance of sisterhood, and about the value in sharing our stories. She was explaining to us that all of us have something that someone needs to hear. Life experiences are worthy of sharing with others to bring healing, wholeness, and resilience to other women who may have experienced the same things. She had just released her first book which chronicled her very transparent journey of a childhood of repeated sexual abuse and trauma. Having the bravery to relive her story exuded strength and courage. Her book reached people in more ways than she even imagined. She asked us to think over our lives about our own story. I sheepishly stood in Carmen's kitchen afraid that I wouldn't have an answer or idea of what my story was. The only thing that came to mind was being adopted. So I said, "I guess I could write about being adopted." Then I thought, yea I'm adopted, so what? How does my adoption look different from anyone else? Who wants to hear about it? What makes mine special? I'm sure there are thousands of books on adoption out there. Who wants to read my book? What if no one buys it? What would the point of the book even be? What message would I want to convey? How vulnerable should I be? What if what I say embarrasses my parents? Writing a book? Where do I start? Who is going to publish it? Does this mean I have to promote my book? Forget it, I'm not doing it. I can't do this. I talked myself out of writing my book in a matter of four and a half minutes. Auntie Bev looked at me directly in my eyes and said, "Do it for Dayna. SHE needs to hear your story." In that moment all of my fear left my body. I had to do it for her. Dayna needed to understand my journey. She deserved to know. With tears brimming in my eyes as my girlfriends stood around me in the center of Carmen's kitchen I said, "I'll do it."

2018 was going to be a new start for me and I wanted to be successful in creating the best me that I could. For me. My new goals were ones that I held myself accountable to. I returned home the next day with a new purpose. I was ready to share my story. I was excited about how I would be used. I was rejuvenated and refreshed. I decided that beginning therapy would be a good idea. I saw a therapist that helped me explore so many feelings

I have had about my life. We did a lot of work and her support allowed me to begin this book writing journey. I was able to make sense of my adoption and how it truly shaped who I am today. Although my feelings towards my biological mother had changed and I was no longer upset with her, talking with a therapist, specifically one who is adoption competent allowed me to unearth some of my communication patterns and behavioral patterns within my relationships with people. I was able to find increased inner peace talking about my adoption as well. It felt good to be in a safe, non-judgmental environment and be able to really explore why I did certain things and felt certain ways growing up. It required transparency and vulnerability, but over time, the sessions empowered me to no longer suffer in silence. Journaling also helped tremendously with healing. It allowed me to identify and clarify my thoughts on being adopted and what that meant for my life. How would I use adoption as a part of my story? Putting the pen to the paper was cathartic. Journaling gave me a tool to look back and see how far I'd come on this journey of healing. I created a space where I owned my feelings and allowed myself to be free in them.

As I began to write my book, I gathered scraps of paper and began to formulate title ideas and chapter names. I began to furiously write every emotion and detail that I could muster up about being adopted. I had to dig deep to really formulate the message I wanted to convey and release feelings that I didn't remember were still inside of me. It required that I put aside all of my fears about things that could go wrong with sharing my story. I had to sit down with my parents and get answers to questions that I wasn't sure I was ready to hear. I had to retrieve my adoption albums and study the content of my documents and pictures again to accurately create a timeline. All of this evoked emotions and thoughts that I have never shared with anyone. Thoughts that were often embarrassing or shameful. Feelings that seemed crazy at times when I felt the most alone. These feelings were ones that I pushed to the very bottom of my mind and hadn't planned on revisiting.

I began to research biographical books on adoption and I didn't see very many from the adoptee perspective. There were a lot of books about adoption and the process. There were tons of articles and blogs about adoption, but I did not see many books. I became hopeful that this book could be different. Maybe an adoptee or adoptive parent could identify their own story through my raw emotion and detailed experiences. When I told my parents I was writing a book I wasn't sure how they would receive it. I was nervous that they would be afraid I would write something that may reflect negatively on my adoption experience. I had to put that feeling aside and allow myself to be truthful and transparent in my own story. I approached them with it, and they were overjoyed. Again, they were willing to help however they could.

It's amazing that I never talked to anyone about any of this growing up. I didn't allow myself to dissect why I felt this way or felt I needed to overcompensate in so many areas of my life. It wasn't until I decided to seek professional help as an adult that I realized that I didn't have to be all things to all people. I didn't need to beat myself up for feeling as if I wasn't enough or that people around me had ill intentions or were going to leave me. I began to recognize that I could just be me and be happy with myself. I had to learn to love myself and identify how much I had to offer. I began to recognize how much love I had to give to people regardless of what I would get in return. I had to distinguish my worth, my value, and trust myself and my feelings with others. I also had to learn to let go of the past and understand that my circumstance did not define my destiny. It was imperative for me to embrace what my life was and what my purpose on this earth was. I had to come to terms with how my life would matter with the life I was given. Once I understood that the feelings I had throughout my life were completely normal, healing began.

My adoption story continues to be a lifelong journey. Every day I learn something new about myself and am thankful for the lessons learned over the years and the mistakes that I made along the way. My parent's decision to adopt me was one that I could never say enough thanks for. They gave me the best life imaginable. They are incredible people who did everything that they could to instill in me that I am loved and I am valued. Who I am today is a direct result of being adopted. I wouldn't change anything about my life. Not one thing. My parents are the best thing that ever happened to me, and I am forever grateful that *they chose me.*

Twelve
EMBRACING YOUR EXPERIENCE

Everyone's adoption experience is unique to them. It is a very real experience. There is nothing that anyone can do to change how the adoptee feels. The emotions are real and they are going to be raw. Our struggle with identity and self-worth is going to be an ongoing cycle. The desire to search for ones biological parents is in no way a rejection of adoptive families. It is just our way of reconnecting with the bond that was severed at the time we were separated from our biological families. It provides a way of reestablishing some sense of identity. Adoption is an experience that spans an entire lifetime. Its impact is lifelong and traumatic. Not every adoptee will be affected by these issues to the same extent. That is what makes adoption and adoptees so special.

As adoptees begin to identify more details of their adoption story and conceptualize their emotions tied to it, they can begin to recognize triggers and establish healthy coping skills and cultivate resilience. Each adoption story is different and the long-term effects of adoption will be different to each adoptee. No two adoption experiences are the same. Some adoptees may never express a desire to learn more about their birth family history and choose not to search for them. Many choose to leave that part of their lives in the past and relish in their present with the families that they have been given. It is perfectly fine for some to be filled with the desire to know, and for others not to have that same yearning. Whatever your decision is, remember to identify a supportive network for yourself.

At times you may feel like a content and well-adjusted adoptee. You may wake up one day and feel like you have it all together; a loving family, great career, bright future, and lots of success. You may truly feel perfectly fine being adopted. But there may be periods in your life that are darker than others. Times where deep down there is an inexplicable grief that begins to slowly pour out little by little. Feelings of sadness and confusion...feelings of guilt and shame. Feelings that you have tried to bury for years and convince yourself that they don't even exist. You may try to persuade yourself that the only feelings you should be experiencing are that of thanksgiving, gratitude, and peace and that you were given a great life by people who truly wanted you. Many will never come to a place of forgiveness for the individuals that abandoned them at hospitals or left them with family members to raise.

Helping adoptees acknowledge this grief by creating an emotional space for this to occur is necessary for healing. This will allow adoptees to move forward in life with healthy relationships, increased feelings of self-worth and value, and establish a sense of identity. Not everyone has a glorious transition through the foster care system. Not everyone is adopted into homes that exude love, support, and acceptance. Many have been placed with vile foster parents who only chose to foster for financial gain. These individuals may have never had any intention to show the abandoned and relinquished child any semblance of love and family. With that, adoptees may experience abandonment all over again.

There are adoptees even after being adopted into what was masked as a loving home, have experienced horrendous acts of sexual, physical, and emotional abuse. Stories of inexcusable trauma directly due to adoption is often present in the form of neglect, and reprehensible hatred have been the theme of the "adoptive family". Other adoptees have recounted times where they were reminded every day that they aren't a true member of the family, and treated like an outsider. Some are made to feel that they are "different" and never felt like they truly belonged. I've seen "memes" on social media that describe adoptees made to feel like an outsider looking into a snowglobe.

Being able to address these feelings with adoptees is important. Understanding that there is a constant search for self and connection is very important. Adoptees often struggle with where they fit in this world. Who can they trust? Will they experience abandonment again? Will they be discarded again? Adoptees separated from their biological mothers as infants will often experience issues of abandonment in a completely different way than those who were cared for by their biological mothers.

I remember needing to feel a sense of control in my relationships with other people to ensure that I wouldn't get hurt. I had a fear of intimacy. I was very distrustful of people and couldn't bear being rejected. However, I didn't have a space to articulate that. Most adopted children won't. How do you bring it up? How does the conversation go? What is supposed to come from it? Most times, children just want to fit in, and not rock the boat. Speaking up about these feelings can be scary. It requires a level of transparency and vulnerability most children don't know how to express. Guilt about the feelings can also be a barrier to initiating these conversations.

Adoptive parents must be honest with themselves about how adoption may be affecting their child. Most adoptive parents just want the child to feel included, welcomed, and a part of the families. Therefore the need for this type of dialogue is often overlooked. Psychological issues directly related to being adopted can be addressed through a therapeutic relationship with a mental health provider. They have the tools to appropriately address issues of abandonment, distrust, low self-esteem, identity issues and depression. These issues may be carried with the adoptee wherever they go, but being able to work through them can help strengthen trust and resilience. Connecting with an adoption competent therapist would be highly beneficial. These therapists will be specifically trained to understand core issues of adoption and appropriately evaluate the needs of the adoptee beginning with their separation from the biological parent.

To Adoptees:

Some of us were confronted with trauma as a direct result of our adoption. Some of us did not have adoptions that we are proud of or thankful for. Some of us still carry a lot of anger and resentment towards the circumstances surrounding our adoptions. I tell you this. You are still in control of rewriting your present and your future. Your circumstances do not define who you are, and you are not a product of your surroundings. You still have the opportunity to invest in yourself with love and fulfill your own destiny. If you are struggling with the many complexities associated with your adoption journey, I implore you to consider counseling as an avenue to explore your feelings. The right therapist can equip you with the proper tools, enabling you to be resilient in your feelings while facilitating the best way to unpack years of questions and pain. Develop a network of support. There are local adoption support groups available filled with people ready to begin their journey of healing. Your desire may be to leave the past in the past. However, your feelings about being adopted may remain, so find a constructive outlet to invest in your journey to healing. You are worth it.

To Adoptive parents:

Your decision to adopt is a bold one. It is a noble responsibility to bring a child into your home and envelop them as a part of your family. There will be days that may be more difficult than others. Your best tool is to listen. Allow your adopted child to emote. Be a presence of support. Allow them to grieve the past that may be unknown to them. However, don't push them to work through feelings that they aren't ready to address. Encourage a dialogue of support to assure them that they are not alone, and that their feelings are in no way an attack on you and the sacrifices you made. Allow them to ask you questions about their adoption and their history. Some of these questions may be accompanied with misconceptions of foster care and the adoption process. This is a great time to facilitate conversation with them regarding their feelings surrounding it all. Find out their understanding about what they know. Be open with them about what you know and remind them that their adoption was simply a step in their life, but it does not define them.

Also, be sure to process your own feelings about the adoption. Taking care of yourself is very important as well. Acknowledging your feelings about the birth parents is also important, so allow yourself to feel. Find a support system for yourself. Adoption support groups are available to adoptive parents to foster a community of peers that are experiencing the adoption journey.

To Birth Parents:

You have already made the bravest decision of your life. You are willing to give your child a second chance. This decision may or may not be an easy one for you. However, birth parents are parents for life. Your decision will come with a host of emotions that you may not expect. It will be imperative for you to attend to your physical recovery from the birth process and emotional recovery postpartum. Childbirth in itself is a very hormonal time. The process can elicit a string of emotions. Some of those may be stronger than others. Surround yourself with people that can support you and your decision. This is crucial. There is a growing network of post placement support services for birth parents that can be made available to you by a simple search within your state. Counseling, support groups, online peer support, and a host of literature can help you during this time. Healing often lasts a lifetime.

A Letter To Mommy

Dear Mommy,

The last time we saw each other was December of 1980. I don't remember it, but I really hope you do. My entire life has been an endless journey of self-discovery. Living life without you has left an incomprehensible emptiness within me. Every day I questioned who I was, why you left me, and what my life with you could have been. I wondered where you were and if you thought about me. I prayed for you often, and hoped you were praying for me.

I wish that there were people who could have convinced you to leave whatever was impairing your ability to be my mom. I'm sorry that your life couldn't accommodate me. I am sorry that there was no one there to stand in for you until you could figure things out, but I thank you for putting me first. For years I didn't see it that way. I bore the weight of anger and resentment towards you. I hated you for leaving me in that hospital. I hated feeling that I wasn't enough for you to choose me. It took a while, but over time I found the strength to forgive you. Forgiving you freed me from the feelings that kept me bound to the past that I had no answers to.

My life has been wonderful. I was given the best family that filled so many of the holes in my heart. They chose me when you made your choice to allow me to have a better life. They have done a fantastic job with me. Their love and support was something I was sure I could only get from you, but I was wrong. God placed them in my life and I am forever grateful to them for all they have done. I am a better person because of them. They remind me of my worth and my value. They constantly sow seeds of affirmation and encouragement into me, cultivating me to be the best person I can be. It is what I needed when I lost you.

I have a family of my own now. They are remarkable. My husband shows me daily what unconditional love is all about. Having my daughter has given me what was taken from me- a biological connection. Looking at her everyday fills me with pride and joy. You would love them. They are truly my favorite people on this Earth.

A LETTER TO MOMMY

I forgive you, mommy. I know you only did what you felt you had to do. For years your decision seemed selfish and callous, but I came to realize that you were only thinking of me. Thank you for that. If we never meet, know that I love you and that I always have. You will always be the vessel that gave me life, and for that, I am forever grateful.

Love always,

JENISE SHACOLE CARTER

They Chose Me

CPSIA information can be obtained
at www.ICGtesting.com
Printed in the USA
LVHW081325160619
621372LV00012B/363/P

9 780578 513362